How to Win by Quitting

How to Win by Quitting

bye
Jerry Stocking

Moose Ear
Press

To correspond with Jerry Stocking or find out about other products offered by Moose Ear Press or A Choice Experience, Inc., see the last page of this book.

Editor: Karen Bates
Copy Editor: Jackie Stocking
Cover design and art work: Dunn & Associates, Inc.

Thank, you, to, Gloria DeWolfe, the comma queen, for her aggressive reading, of the manuscript,. Thank you also to Eric Stromquist and Dean Franklin for their unflagging support over the years.

Published by
Moose Ear Press
First Printing 1997

ISBN: 0-9629593-5-9

TABLE OF CONTENTS

Section One
How to Win By Quitting

CONTENTS

Section Two
A Piece of Cake

Preface

It took several days to build a chicken coop for my daughter's fifty baby chickens. Once the chickens were in their new house, we ran chicken wire around an enclosed area, building a playground where they could explore and expand their world. I should have taken note of the chickens' behavior earlier. Upon entering their new coop, they huddled in one corner, and ventured out only when they were very thirsty or hungry. Triumphantly, I opened the front door of the coop, once the fence was up. No chicken ventured out. Perhaps they didn't understand what I had done for them. Perhaps they didn't know that in contrast to the confinement of their new house they were free, free to stretch their legs and run around, free to enter the sunlight for the first time and feel a breeze on their little beaks or combs.

I couldn't set the chickens free; they huddled together, confining themselves into the smallest area that fifty baby chickens would fit into. With their entirely programmed little brains, they were not able to be free; only in my perception did freedom look like a large area to wander. To them, life, and perhaps safety, looked like the smallest area possible, huddled together with nothing to explore, and very little movement necessary or possible. At first, I was angry with the chicks. I had worked so hard to let them go, but they wouldn't be released. I even raised my voice; they huddled more closely. I pushed a couple of chicks out the door, lightly. They immediately went under the coop, a dark and dirt filled place much more restrictive than the coop. It was very difficult to get them out of their new hiding place. Finally, I understood; the chickens couldn't understand. It isn't possible to set someone free who doesn't want to be. Trapped is a state of mind. The chickens were trapped by their evolutionary position, programmed from birth to death. There was not to be a moment of liberation for them, no epiphany of release.

For years, I had been puzzled by the behavior of people in workshops. I would show them how to be free, and they wouldn't accept it. They would huddle together, safe perhaps, certainly in hiding. When it is time to be free, when you are ready to be free, you will do what is necessary to be free. Freedom is not your birthright; you must set yourself free, because it is you who oppresses yourself. You are the problem and the solution, the ruler and the one who is ruled; you are free but don't know you are. Until you can be entirely oppressed, you cannot be free. If you are free, there will be nothing that you have to think or have to do. Nothing will be mandatory for you. This is a free country, but ironically nobody is free, almost nobody. I invite you to use quitting as a tool to set yourself free.

Q

My son, age three, almost four, was falling asleep on my lap. Hundreds of times, I had watched him fall asleep. He usually held his eyes open until he fell asleep. This time I asked him about it. I suggested that he close his eyes and go to sleep. He replied, "I wouldn't want to hurt my eyes by forcing them closed. When my eyes close, I fall asleep; I just wait until they close." My son is not the least bit passive, but he trusts; he is patient enough to take and to appreciate what comes when it comes. Occasionally, his world falls apart, as he tries to have things be a certain way. He tries to force the universe to yield to his wishes. The results of such behaviors in a three-year-old are obvious and traumatic, but, in an adult, they are so commonplace they are life itself. Do nothing, and you will discover what unfolds. You will discover your perfection, all the time, everywhere. You will return to the innocence of a child, and you won't have to control the universe. Earth is either a playground or a torture chamber; your perspective determines which. If you think that it is sometimes wonderful, and sometimes awful or always awful, you have forfeited the wonder and mystery that can be yours, always. If you settle for something, you won't think you deserve everything. Earth is your playground. Let your eyes close when they do and open when they do. When they open, look on Earth anew, for the first time, the best present that you can currently accept. Accept it.

Introduction

Life for many people is empty. Walk down the street and look at peoples faces; are they happy? Watch the evening news, but only once please; how much of it is good news? Calculate the divorce rate. Walk through a town after dark, and notice how many house interiors are illuminated by the glow of television sets. It doesn't matter what you buy, you aren't happy, but you go on working to buy more. So many people want jobs other than the ones they have. If you have kids, it is easier to give them anything except time with you. So many people are sick. Drugs are rampant, legal and illegal. How many women in this country are on some kind of anti-depressant drug?

How much of your day is consumed by what you perceive you have to do? Nobody works well under slave conditions. When you give up your right to quit, you give up your freedom. You don't become a quitter when you quit—you just quit. We are a nation of addicts. The obvious addicts need the needle, and the less obvious need to be busy. Anytime you identify who you are by something other than everything, you have lost.

As young children, the training begins. Children play games and are taught that they may win or they may lose, but they must never quit. To quit just to quit is unthinkable. Quitting brings into question the very existence and importance of any game. Quitting is a threat that games will not survive for long. The essence of a game, all games, is that what isn't is considered more important than what is. While this is philosophical suicide, it is also worse than that. It alienates people from all that is, including themselves. It has people lose everything, and then think that if they work hard enough, they just might gain part of it back. They give up trying for even a part of everything, and just keep working hard. People learn that they must play (compete, struggle, and finally win or lose), whether they like it or not. Within all games, you will lose. The very act of playing a game guarantees that you lose.

Even the people who are quitting do so with a taboo against it. They make up reasons, and, even with good reasons, they still get wounded in the process of quitting.

It is time to quit. To legitimatize quitting. To remove the old, typically unspoken, taboo against quitting. Don't quit for a reason, just quit to find out what the result of quitting is. If you quit doing something that you perceive you must do, you soon discover that you didn't have to do it at all. Slaves can't quit—free people can. Can you?

When you quit what you perceive you have to do, you will discover what you want to do. The quality of work is much better when people are doing what they want to do, rather than what they have to do. I am not suggesting that you do nothing. I am suggesting that anything you perceive you *must* do ruins your life. Quitting can lead you to discovering who you are, rather than who you perceive yourself to be or some version of what you do or own.

Quitting will make you smarter and happier. It really will. It doesn't matter what you are doing; if you can't quit, you are not free. Slavery was abolished many years ago, but it is alive and well, flourishing and institutionalized in workplaces across America. If the slaves discover that they can be free, they will seldom remain enslaved. The taboo against quitting has made you a slave, and you probably don't even know it. The rules of the games you are playing are driving you crazy. As you quit the games, you will become sane. The therapists don't want you to quit. The drug companies don't want you to quit. Big business, which depends on your purchases, doesn't want you to quit. Nobody wants you to quit. But that is just because quitting is a threat to how things are. Most people and institutions will always be defending how things are, otherwise they wouldn't be this way. As individuals quit, and discover what being free is like, others will catch on;

and after enough people quit, the institutions will discover how to make money and survive without feeding on the suffering and enslavement of people.

What would life be like if you could do exactly what you wanted to, all of the time? That is what life becomes for someone who has quit often enough. Creativity arises out of quitting; you can make up games that work. Laziness is not playing the game from within the structure of the game; quitting is something else entirely. Staying in games that you don't enjoy, or that are not rewarding, just because you have always done it or because you get paid to do it or because others are doing it, will squeeze the life out of your life. The promise of this country is freedom, but there are very few free people around. Anyone who perceives that they must work is no more free than someone who must inject heroin. It doesn't matter what you are addicted to, addiction is offensive to the spirit, and it ends freedom. The definition of addiction is not being able to quit.

Read this book and quit anytime you want to, but then perhaps pick it up and read some more. With some luck, and a bit of bravery on your part, you will reach within and discover that you can be free, that quitting can set you free. Quitting will set you free. It is never too early to quit, and it is never too late to quit. When you quit it is now.

1

Quitting Work

 I vividly recall sitting at my desk at Shearson Lehman Brothers. The decision had just been made—I was going to resign within one month. My affairs were not in order, but I suspected that they might never get organized sufficiently to justify waiting for them. Quitting a really good job where I was making money, plenty of money, and had no complaints was in the same class as suicide. Over the past several years I had proved that I could do the job. Initially, I had broken all sales records, and then settled into a pace of production that could easily have resulted in financial comfort for myself, my wife, and my newborn daughter. No one wanted me to quit. My branch manager could not even consider the possibility of having me quit. The other brokers in the office often spoke about quitting, but only as a technique to show the unacceptable consequences of leaving such a "good" job, and to pretend they could quit if they wanted to. My parents were too polite and intelligent to get involved in my career, so I had to make up what their response would be to my throwing away the security of a good, steady income for no certain money at all. Particularly, society didn't want me to quit. "If you have a good job hold on to it, for heaven's sake." My daughter was not yet old enough to speak for herself, so I had to make up her opinion. My wife was interested, but impressively willing to let me decide for myself, even though the decision would affect her future. I guess the *nobody* who didn't want me to quit was primarily a cultural force.

I had numerous careers before becoming a stockbroker, any one of which could have lasted a lifetime. I had been a retail store owner, an industrial designer, and a purveyor of limited partnerships. In each of these pursuits I had been successful, but always moved on to yet another career with greater challenges, more pressure and more status. I was on the career ladder and climbing, paying more attention to the ladder than whatever it might be leaning on. Henry David Thoreau was the only role model I knew for what I was about to do, and being forced to read him in high school had aroused my disinterest sufficiently that he influenced me little. I was getting older and wearing myself out doing things every day that I would not have done if monetary recompense had not been forthcoming. I was selling myself for money. I did not yet realize that money is an excuse, a story one tells oneself to remain in an intolerable or just plain uninspirational situation. Money never inspires anyone, though it appears to. Inspiration comes from deep within, from a place that money cannot touch. I was a prostitute who didn't think he was one.

Quitting wasn't easy. It is easier to do something that makes sense. To do something that everybody else is doing. To do something that one gets paid for. To do something that one can explain in a sentence or two.

I balked. Surely I had to have some other job before I quit this one. What about my daughter, how would I support her? I interviewed with two different branch managers for related jobs on the next rung of the ladder. I spoke to a past employer who wanted to hire me back. No, I discovered that jumping from something to something else is not the same as jumping from something to nothing. I had to quit and remain uncertain of what I would do next; to do otherwise would be an end run around the trust that a leap into the void required. In every situation there are ways to learn more and ways to learn less. The safest, usually most sensible path is the one that will teach you the least. While I was in the financial services business I was trapped, and I found myself looking for other jobs in that business. I did not yet know how to clean my slate so that I could write my future independent of the past, and trust myself to find exactly what I ought to do. I had to quit—cold turkey. No more interviews. Put my affairs in the best order possible and just quit.

Unable to see my own face at the time, I vividly remember the culmination of all the torment of quitting this job—the look on my branch manager's face. Incredulous, he could not believe what he was hearing. "You can't quit. You're kidding." Surely I would follow in his footsteps. Certainly the big money ahead justified staying. Didn't I want to grow up to be just like him? Why was I leaving? Story time. Tell him that I was going to a competitor. Tell him anything that would have him make sense of what he was hearing. There was nothing to say. I was quitting because I still could. I was moving on to greener or browner or totally uncertain pastures. I was giving up the certain for the call of the uncertain. I thanked him for the support that he had given me over the years and quit.

Walking back to my office for the last time, the other brokers did not look as they had before. They had been necessary parts of my day, now they looked ridiculous. There was Jim, lying to someone on the phone to get them to sell one stock and jump into another. There was Art, the office powder keg, who at least once a week would break into an immature temper tantrum that would result in his throwing things and screaming at anyone within earshot. Allen, sitting at his quotron machine still thinking that somehow his intellect drove the market. Dennis was trading options, a moment to moment existence, waiting to discover how much his clients had lost that day. These people were not happy, they didn't even ponder the possibility of happiness. They were each running their own little torture chamber justified by the American Dream. Each was seeking fortune in a contrived and pathetic environment. Most of them ate too much, many of them drank too much, and some of them had illegal habits I'd rather not even think about. In other words, this was a typical office, one in which I would play no more. Yet, in spite of this, quitting was one of the most difficult things I have ever done. For years afterward, I had bad dreams about it. I had been taught from an early age, as I suspect most of us had, that quitting is losing. Winners never quit and quitters never win.

Having become a successful predator, this day marked the resignation of my role in the food chain. Competition let one know where one stood. My older brother, by two years, never let me miss that lesson. Little league, school, tag were important instructors at the school of competition. Looking back, almost everything I did was based on competition, though often it didn't seem like it at the time. As a brother, I competed for my parents' attention. As a student, every other member of the class was my adversary. In every situation there seemed to be better and worse outcomes and I, of course, wanted the better. The idea of not playing was a threat, "I will take my ball and go home," that was never taken seriously. Quitting was impossible, everybody knew that, though occasionally it worked as a ploy. "I quit," is an un-American expression.

What do you mean, "You quit?" You can't quit. As long as you are alive you must be playing. Everybody needs a job. Everybody must take the Iowa Basic Achievement Test. Everybody must continually compare themselves to others. In order to have order we must define that order and we must always keep order. Are you in the top or the bottom of your class? Did you win the game? What position do you play? Where is your brother? Who did you go to the dance with? What do you do? How do you do?

Where do you live? What does your father do? Let me see your report card.

Everything in my life, it seemed, was geared to discovering just how good or how bad I was on some scale that was not even specified exactly. At what point does a thermometer register warm as opposed to cold? We supposedly live in a scientific age, and yet the techniques we use to judge our children, ourselves, or other people are hardly objective. The thermometer doesn't care what the temperature is. It doesn't prefer the readings above zero to the ones below. People have preferences for almost everything. I can't think of a persistent exception, and they judge themselves by those often changing preferences. The bar height keeps changing, but who is moving the bar? Is it good to jump higher, and bad to jump lower? How high is high enough? We constantly, compulsively measure ourselves. We want to know where we stand in relation to all there is. Specifically, we want to know just how good and just how bad we are. We would rather be bad and know it than be uncertain about whether we are good or bad.

We engage in competitive games each and every day, games that are so hooked to life that we see life through them. They have become reality for us. A social worker once said to me, "You are so competitive." In other words, she was better than I because she was less competitive than I was. I guess she won the competition to be the least competitive. Competition is sneaky; when you least expect it, or don't recognize it, competition puts you in your place, or more accurately, it puts you *some* place and calls that place *your* place. The social worker upped the stakes, she competed to be the least competitive, but I showed her, we never went out again. Who won?

"Who won?" Sometimes the question is blatant, often covert. If I called a client and they bought the stock I was pitching then I won, but somebody had to lose. I guess the client lost. If I asked a woman out on a date, and she declined, then she won and I lost. But, if she accepted, then I won and she lost. Which meant that I was going out with a loser. As Woody Allen said, "I wouldn't want to join a group that would have me as a member." Competition is like that, it ties you up in the game where winning and losing is always important and seldom obvious.

Q

When I was about ten I started to play tennis. I was an immediate success. In my first tennis lesson, the instructor told me that I was a natural tennis player and that I really should be playing competitive tennis. My first lesson was through a local park and I was better than any of the people in the class. I was proud of myself. I practiced and learned everything I could about playing tennis. The beginning of my second summer of tennis found me ready for a bigger challenge.

I headed across town, on my bike, to a high school where they had a tennis ladder. There were about forty people who were ranked in order on the ladder. I was very excited to play my first competitive game and to be ranked according to other players. As luck would have it, that day the competition was set randomly. Names were drawn out of a tennis hat to find out who played whom. I had my opponent chosen. He was a short fat guy, and I figured that I wouldn't have much trouble with him. If I beat him, I got to be at his spot on the ladder. After hitting a few balls with him to warm up, I knew I was in trouble. He swung his racquet easily and gracefully. He covered the court faster than anyone I had ever seen. During our match he did not have to cover the court much. He could place the ball right where he wanted to every time. I ran and ran and ran. The final score was six to zero in his favor. He was ranked number two on the ladder, and the following school year he went on to win one of the top spots in the state of Illinois.

With my tennis career in perspective, I continued to play. It would be great if I could tell you that one day I played him again and beat him. I never did play him again and doubt that I ever would have beaten him. I had been taught a lesson that day. I thought I was a great tennis player, when I compared myself to lesser players. While I was playing the number two player, I didn't know that he was number two so I was embarrassed and upset at being beaten by such a fat little boy. I was so busy being upset, I lost a great opportunity to learn more about the game of tennis from a good player.

There were numerous other opportunities in my tennis playing years in which I beat people much better than me and sometimes lost to people much worse than me. I never forgot the lessons I learned that summer day, that I had better enjoy myself no matter what I was doing because, if I enjoyed myself, that made me the winner and the people around me winners as well; and that no matter what you do, there are people better than you and worse than you, but the only person you have to please is yourself. Tennis was fun for me when I improved; I had determined improvement to be important. If I had decided that winning was important to my happiness, I only would have had to focus on the players worse than myself. If I wanted to be sad, I could find players better than me. It was all a matter of perspective, but I was not dependent on perspective unless I let myself be.

One way out of this game is to claim that everybody wins or everybody loses, the classic optimist versus pessimist competition, but still it is competition. Rooted in competition, somebody has to win and somebody has to lose; that is the nature of the game we have made up and become slaves to. We want to know where we stand and are willing to lose or beat up somebody else to find out. Beat up—all that means is that you get up before they do. Pretend that you are a particularly aggressive well-paid member of our culture and you have invested a week's pay to get a front row seat at an "important" boxing match. This is a title fight, both fighters are champions, but one is better than the other, and their reputations and futures are riding on this fight. You don't realize that your reputation and future is riding on it too, but they always are in a competitive paradigm. Tension and excitement build as the boxers make their way to the ring. The crowd goes wild as one boxer bumps the other aggressively during the rules talk. Finally, the moment you have waited for, the moment you paid for, the moment that will determine the world champion of boxing arrives. The bell rings and the boxers erupt from their corners, run at each other, collide, and both are rendered unconscious for two days.

Isn't it frustrating not to know who won and who lost? The bookies don't know what to do. Do they void the bets and refund the money? Who won? Who lost? Where do you stand? You went to the fight to be entertained, but primarily to be one of the first to find out who won and who lost. You have to identify with one of the boxers whether he wins or loses.

I walked out of Shearson Lehman Brothers that day, carrying a cardboard box containing some personal belongings. I was neither satisfied nor unsatisfied. I was awake, alert, and I had no idea what would come next. I walked lightly, freely to my car and drove home, where I was greeted by my wife and had the opportunity to play with my daughter. This was different from the Friday afternoons I spent knowing I would be back to work on Monday. Like someone fasting for the first time and discovering how often they think about food, I began to discover how much my work had defined me. Even on weekends I had still been a stockbroker.

I gave up knowing where I stood for standing where I stood in the moment. I gave up competing to be the best broker in the office, selling the most stock, or being the "good" bread winner. I quit. And when I quit, my life outside the loop almost began. Almost, because it took me a while to realize that I really didn't need to go in to work the next day. Now I could do exactly what I wanted each moment. Freedom is an incomprehensible idea to people who have learned from an early age how to oppress themselves. Freedom is the ability to quit. I was thirty-eight years old and had quit.

I quit, and resisted the temptation to engage in the, "Now what?" conversation. I was out of the loop and didn't even know who I was. The only alternative I perceived was to redefine myself.

It would be years before I could escape my competitive past. Culture pushes and pulls, it shoves, it beckons. It took years to gain perspective and look at what we call life that isn't life at all. I had to gain the wisdom to untangle the unimportant from the important, the accessories from the functional. A different intelligence is necessary for untangling than that used for tangling. My suits are still hanging in a row, only now they reside in the attic next to my Allen Edmonds shoes.

You must behave in a reality before you can perceive in that reality. I behaved—quit—and my new reality began.

2

"Thou Shalt Work"

What if you were always satisfied? What if you were totally and completely fulfilled, fearless, and far beyond happy? What if you were guaranteed this satisfaction forever, if you could not escape it no matter how hard you tried? (And you try so hard, to be good, to do the right thing, to ascend in such noble ways.) What would life be like if you began it whole, complete, and omnipotent rather than spending your life struggling to reach these ideals?

You are engaged in many games: the husband-wife game, the employment game, the parent game, the son-daughter game, the get ahead game, the look good game, and many more. You know some of the objectives and a few of the rules, but so few of both that for the most part you are playing blind. In order to rise above the game, rather than playing compulsively, you have to quit. Quitting will allow you to begin to see all of the objectives and rules and discern whether these are games you really wish to play.

Through the bars of your cell, the world looks different than it would without bars. It isn't nice or polite to say it, but you are trapped, controlled, and driven in ways you never chose and don't recognize. There are assumptions, facts, you perceive as life, which are fabrications and illusions. There are no *real* facts but, trapped as you are, you can't see this.

The chickadee visits the window of the condemned man's cell every day. The man feeds it bread crumbs and vicariously takes flight each time the chickadee flies away. The man attempts to ignore the inevitable death sentence (ours). He thinks about dying—a release from this prison. If he were free, dying would be unthinkably painful but from this cell it is easier. He trains the bird to land on his hand. It is so light. Black helmet. Tender song. At first the chickadee perches on the man's hand but gradually it becomes willing to be held snugly in the dark chamber formed by the man's cupped hands. Each day, for a crust of bread, he stays in his small dark enclosure longer. The man's love, first love, increases as the bird joins him in his captivity. Each day he keeps his love with him longer and closes his hands more tightly.

The chickadee was never free; he needs the bread. He has lost nothing, can lose nothing, and has gained a friend, a lover. One day he flies to the window sill and there is no bread and no man, and he flies to the window of another cell and another. He has a job.

The man escaped, to death or resurrection; either way he misses the bird, longs for its company, and has moved full cycle from the future to the past. The chickadee was never free. Freedom requires an escape from patterns which the bird's tiny brain cannot accomplish. The man could be free, open to all possibilities, but will he be?

Once out, nothing looks the same. Has everything changed? I wake up in the morning to the sound of house sparrows. It is early, though it seems I have slept in. I can still make it to work on time. I arise to the sounds of my wife playing with my daughter in the kitchen. I shower and dress quickly, thinking of little but knowing what I must do. My wife smiles at me in my suit and asks if perhaps I have overdressed for my first day of retirement. How many more mornings will I get up and forget that I don't have to go to work? Habit—the great unequalizer has struck again. The repetition necessary for habit robs people of so many waking moments that they seem to be asleep. Anytime you are engaged in movement from one particular moment to another particular moment, you miss all of the moments in between. Transit times become greater as you become a waiter without tips. You wait for the right moment which must make this the wrong moment. I smile, embarrassed, another carryover from a world where right and wrong reign, where it is wrong to forget that I quit. You too quit, or never started playing, but you keep forgetting and getting hooked back into the game. I grab my tie, pull it up over my head in a gesture meant to symbolize being hung by the symbols of work. I drop to my knees and begin to play with my daughter, something that I would not have done if I needed to go to work.

A half hour goes by as we play. It is time to change into sweatpants and a T-shirt. In one way I am more comfortable, and in the other I will not be until I hurry to get my day planned. But, there is no planning to do. There is nothing to do. There are no plans to make and no appointments to keep. It doesn't even matter what the market is doing. I alternately talk with my wife about nothing and play with my daughter, who seems to so thoroughly enjoy her own company all she needs is somebody watching, and ready. The phone rings, a reprieve; perhaps it is something which demands my much too plentiful attention. Wrong number, or perhaps somebody trying to have us change phone companies, no activity required. The first day passes, the longest until the second day arrives. I must do something because I am losing track of who I am. I am disappearing, or at least all that I have considered myself to be is leaving.

I am too young to have this problem. Can't it wait until sixty-five and mandatory retirement? Those of you who have worked long and hard and then retired know what I mean. You are what you do in this culture, even more than you are what you own. Since I am doing nothing then I must be nothing. Later, it became apparent that inadvertently I had discovered one of the most important doors to reality—nothing. Everybody ought to practice retirement every few years. As the days crawled on I continued to evade distraction. The temptation was to look for a job, go back to my former job, or at least volunteer somewhere to keep myself busy. The primary addiction of human beings in this culture is staying busy. Everybody, anybody will fight for your right to work but who will fight for your right not to work?

There is no right not to work. One of the basic assumptions of our culture is that you are good if you are working, and bad, unworthy or pitiful if you are not working. If you are unemployed then you had better at least be complaining about not working, and you should be looking for work. It doesn't even matter if you are making much money as long as you are working. If you are working so hard that you are always busy then you are even better. Rule number one in this culture, a very superficial rule at that, is, "Thou shalt work." If you break this rule you become suspect and worthless unless you have a good enough story to justify your lack of gainful employment, then you will just be worthless. If you are badly injured and can't work, then you become an invalid which makes you invalid. Any excuses for not working other than a short vacation, a sabbatical, retirement, or medical reasons, are unacceptable.

I had accidentally butted up against the number one cultural rule the moment I considered quitting without immediately starting another job. The rule is tyrannical. Many people work because they cannot consider not working, which is too painful and punished too thoroughly to risk. "Thou shalt work." You must work until you fall over dead, reach a certain age, or are disabled.

How prevalent is this rule? How unquestioned? Look at your own life to find out. How much of your life after age eighteen or college have you spent unemployed in some form or other? Ask the people around you the same question and you will quickly discover that you have to work.

People don't work for money, though they pretend they do. They work to work. People who win the lottery go on working. People who have more money than they can spend in their lifetime go on working. People who inherit bags of money continue to work in some form or another. Why? Because, "Thou shalt work."

Working occupies your time; it fills your life. It gives you something to talk to people about. It gives you a place to go and people to see. It gives you an answer to the question, "What do you do?" Working puts meaning in your life. You are worth something because you are working. You mean something. Without work your life would be empty and meaningless. You would have no motivation to do anything. Working defines a shallow empty life. You never discover who you are or what you can do. If you have to have a job, and you have to have it quickly, then you are under pressure to make a decision about work. If you doubt the pressure, just consider how many times children get asked what they want to be when they grow up. I bet you have even asked that question of some defenseless child. Children must learn the rules. The sooner we get them working, cleaning their rooms, doing the chores, going to school, the sooner they will learn what life is really about. They have to learn how to perform tricks and get rewards. If you eat your vegetables you can have dessert. Vegetables become work. If you clean your room you can have an allowance. Children learn early that they must work. We teach them the importance of work by leaving them for long periods of time, even while they are very young, just to do our work. If we are particularly crazy, we claim to be leaving the child for the child's sake, to put a roof over his or her head or food on the table or to buy the latest special toy which represents our love.

It is not your fault that you have to work. It is the rule, "Thou shalt work," that is at fault. Centuries ago thou didn't have to work. Thou could sit around and think, if thou were of a certain class. Thou could explore the human condition, really think free of economic constraints, free from the rule. Socrates worked part time at the public baths, Plato worked at McDonalds to help support his studies. No they didn't. The rule, "Thou shalt work," was not in force back then except for the slaves and underclass who were forced to work. We have all joined the underclass, become members of the working class by obeying the "Thou shalt work" rule. We have given up time to think, read, or play, and replaced it with time to work.

One of the very odd things about "Thou shalt work" is that it is so much a part of our culture that it seems ridiculous or radical to even question it. Somehow Thoreau got away with questioning it. Of course everybody must work, or maybe not. I didn't go into work and became very curious about what would happen next. What would free time reveal to me that enslavement did not? Would I shrivel up and die without work, or would I prosper and discover exactly what I ought to be doing outside of a model that demanded work?

3

The Carnival

Imagine that you are a young child at your first carnival, and you are very excited. You notice rather quickly that if you want to go on rides or buy things you will need money. Nothing is free, at least not anything of supposed value. Luckily you have brought all of your money with you. In your pocket you have a five dollar bill, four quarters, two nickels and eleven pennies. At your tender age this seems like all of the money in the world, until you begin to understand that you can't ride all of the rides with that amount of money. While the carnival is supposed to be fun it has just taught you one of the cruelest lessons in life, that you are limited. You recall your delight with your wealth when at home, but here at the carnival each ride costs at least a dollar. You realize that you must be selective. You must budget your money and deny yourself most of the rides. Now the carnival does not seem like such a nice place. It points out your shortcomings without providing a solution for them. You start to wonder which rides you want to spend your money on. This puts a burden on you, and it puts a burden on the rides, in that you begin to build expectations about getting your money's worth, since the ride you are on has robbed you of the opportunity of taking some other ride. The ride you are on becomes an obstacle. That's no way to have fun!

Luckily, maybe, you find a refreshment stand where you notice a mountain of unwashed cooking pots. You offer to wash the pots, for a price. The woman who owns the stand agrees to hire you, and you begin to work. Three hours later you have washed all of the pots, and the woman gives you five dollars. You are very pleased with yourself. You have almost doubled the number of rides you can go on. What you fail to notice is that you had come to the carnival for a good time and thus far you have discovered the concept of limitation, had your fortune appear small, and put yourself to work.

This is such a great carnival with so many rides that you soon realize you don't yet have enough money for all of them. You decide to ride on a particularly scary looking roller coaster. As you are riding, instead of just enjoying yourself, you notice from the high points of the coaster that there are other rides that might even be more fun than the one you are on. You can hardly wait to finish the roller coaster so you can get to the other rides. You count your money as you think about which one you want to do next. It is strange that you still have more money than you came with and yet it seems to be not enough. You don't dare do another ride for fear of having too little money. You are in luck, maybe; this is such a busy day at the fair that the concession stand you worked at before has another pile of dirty pans. You clean the pans and enter into a deal with the woman who owns it that you will clean the pans for her whenever they get dirty. You are glad you started your day at the carnival early because you have worked and worried the day into early evening. It starts to get dark; you wish it were getting dark from rain and not from impending night. But your day is coming to a close, and you are tired and hungry. The woman sells you a hot dog and some onion rings for half price and you sit down to your dinner. By the time you have finished eating, it is dark and you have only enough time and energy for one more ride. You can't decide which ride to take until it is almost too late. You finally decide on some bumper cars; they look like fun, they don't cost too much, and you are sure you won't see any other tempting rides while you ride them. You take your drive and head home as they are closing the carnival for the day. You drag yourself home, tired, disillusioned (illusioned) and dirty.

Your mother is waiting for you at the door. She asks you if you had a good day. You break into tears and are unable to explain to her why you are crying. Between tears, you ask her if you can go back to the carnival the next day because you have gotten a job, one that must be done and that you do well. She asks you how the rides were, and you break out in tears again.

Repeat your carnival day often enough and it becomes a typical day. Maybe you are not really a kid anymore; maybe you have grown up. Maybe this is all there is to life, though you doubt it. Day after day you go back to the carnival, take a ride occasionally, but mostly you work. You earn money but it is never enough, and you long for the day when you could still cry about your predicament.

4

"Thou Shalt Watch TV"

As I sat in my LazyBoy recliner, I received numerous invitations. Things I could do became obvious to me. The moment that I did nothing there seemed to be so much to do, but somehow not having to go to work allowed me to notice that I really didn't have to do anything.

The television called quietly to me. It knew how to tempt me. I turned it on and two hours of my long day disappeared. What happened to those two hours? What didn't happen was obvious. I had not been with my wife or daughter, the two people whom I cared most about in the world, and I had missed the opportunity to get to know more about myself. I wasn't sure how much I cared for myself. It had been several days since I had earned any money, and I was now uncertain about my worth.

The television passively beckoned to me, silently promising to shorten my days and connect me with millions of other people also watching TV. The average American watches about six hours of television per day; here was my chance to be above average. I could watch for seven hours, eight, or even more. I don't think I made the quota of six hours per day, but I didn't quit television either, at least not at first. It took me two years of experimental retirement before I was able to quit watching television. Looking back, it would have been fruitful to quit sooner, but I couldn't. It isn't necessarily the second rule in this culture, but near the top of the rules is, "Thou shalt watch TV."

School kids talk about television. Adults depend on television. You can always watch television until you have to go to bed so that you can get up and go to work the next day. This may sound a little critical, sorry; it is just that as a watcher of television it seemed to be worth watching. Now, after seven years without TV it looks like a big waste of time. People watch TV to have company before work, to unwind after work, and to lull themselves to sleep at night. TV is a drug, more pervasive than any other drug we have. It is a legal untaxed drug. Television eats time, and is a tool to ensure that you don't learn about yourself. Let's watch TV for a moment.

You arrive home from work and turn on the evening news. You sit down on the couch with a drink, to find out what happened in the world-at-large today. Your mind is numbed by the drink but even more so by watching a series of lights dance across a screen on the front of a box.

You sit and watch the box. You sit passively, not moving your head, not thinking, transfixed by the movements on the screen accompanied by sound. You make sense of the colors on the screen, you form them into images in your head. Try sitting that still sometime with the television off. It isn't easy. The television hypnotizes you. You are in a trance and you have left yourself behind. This is called relaxation. On the screen you see people getting shot in places you will never go. You see all kinds of things that are of interest to you only because they are brought to you in this little box, and may assist you in communication with others tomorrow at work. Television stunts your growth and makes you dumber. The only way to win the wrestling match with a television is to quit watching. Like any addiction it will not be easy to quit, at first, but not long afterward you will realize the extent to which that box was running and ruining your life. How many shootings have you seen other than on the TV? If you have seen one you are in a small minority, and you discovered that it was not like it is portrayed on TV. It is shocking and sickening. It is real. Television makes illusion real and makes reality appear illusionary. It replaces the three dimensions of the world with a flat two-dimensional representation. The mind does the rest, in that what you saw on TV soon becomes as much a part of your thinking as what really happened to you. TV no longer is a part of life, it is life. If you are still watching TV, it will probably sound to you as if I am overstating its effects. If you quit for a few years, what I am saying will become obvious.

Q

Jenny finally got her dream job. She had proven herself as a secretary, she had almost completed college but she had always been torn between her work, what she had to do, and watching television, what she wanted to do. Her dream job was getting paid to watch television. Did you ever hear statistics about how many murders, violent acts, or sexual situations occur on television daily? Jenny's job was to keep track of those three events as they unfolded on the screen. Her shift was to watch channel five from 9:00am to 5:00pm with an hour for lunch, seven total hours watching the set. She was already one hour above average. While she was doing her job, she would record her favorite soap operas from other channels so she could watch them in the evening. The days passed, the days of our lives, and Jenny did her job. She became so immersed in television that she was hesitant to ever leave the house. Her social life became activities on the tube. When there was a marriage, she was getting married. This week she was beaten up seven times, got seduced three times, was pregnant once, was fired twice, and that was only on work time. In the evening she partook in more vicarious fun. Of course Jenny put on weight because she had to snack while she was watching. As she became larger, it became easier and easier to justify remaining seated. Jenny's idea of a hero, other than all of her TV idols, was the inventor of the remote control.

Q

Not every journey is difficult and not every trip is easy; there are infinite possibilities between the poles of each dichotomy. None of these are real; they are a matter of the disposition and perceptual limitations of the traveler. What is delightful for one can be difficult for another. For the more flexible traveler, a situation can be both delightful and difficult at the same time.

Benny was ready for a journey despite some conversations he had to the contrary. He had prepared his whole life for this moment; he was ready if reluctant. He pondered the trip ahead from many different perspectives. In his mind he could think that the journey was already done, could consider possible endings, and ponder what he might do on his journey to facilitate one ending over another.

There he was, deep in thought. His body was ready but his mind was fearful. No matter how small the journey there is the possibility of going astray, of running into someone or something that was not anticipated and having to instantaneously respond in some unprepared way. There are always dangers in new terrain, as Benny was all too aware. He thought back to other trips he had taken. Surprisingly, he thought about a school field trip when he was in eighth grade. He recalled that the whole trip was planned out in such detail by the teacher that though it was a safe trip it was not much fun. Uncertainty seems to reach deep within a person and arouse the energy one calls fun or happy. The unknown is both more frightening and more enjoyable than the known. The organized field trip had been to the art institute, one of his first exposures to fine art. The teacher had scheduled the event so thoroughly by her own tastes that she knew exactly which pictures the children should see and for how long they should view each one. The companion list to her "must see" artwork was a much longer list of art that was either not good enough or in some way too offensive for the children to see. Rubens was definitely on the "to avoid" list, while some of the more conservative old masters and Norman Rockwell were on the "must see" list. It seemed the teacher had always had one major ambition in life and that was to be a model for a Norman Rockwell painting.

It was a dull field trip, and the students soon learned that the teacher had not included fun in their schedule. But the teacher's strategy backfired and, although Benny temporarily lost all interest in art, it was a very eventful trip. Children will not abide by the dull and uninteresting for long, and these children were no exception. If they had known more about the wonderful world of art, they could have sneaked off and viewed some truly radical paintings, but they did not. In lieu of this knowledge, they began to look at each other for excitement and delight. Given their age and hormones, the boys looked at the girls and the girls looked at or pretended not to look at the boys. The teacher looked at the art and their schedule, but not in that order.

During school, the students were usually kept busy and disciplined when they were allowed to interact together. There were rules to thwart attempts at intimacy.

Children are naturally intimate until they learn not to be, and Benny was ready. He had not noticed Charlene before, though she had watched him occasionally. She was a better student than he was but that didn't deter him. There was something about her that spoke to him in a deep primitive language that he could not understand but couldn't resist responding to.

One thing led to another as it always does, and the art institute went down in Benny's history as the scene of his first kiss. Awkward, daring, exciting, and oh so unforgettable. Love for the first time sealed with such an awkward gesture. He had seen plenty of people kissing, especially on television, but when it came to doing it himself it was nothing like those witnessed kisses. Benny wondered if it was so wonderful and unique for others; he especially wondered how it was for Charlene. It was a full five minutes of wonder and four paintings later that the effects of his first kiss settled enough for him to want another. He found that first kiss more addictive than potato chips. The second kiss didn't happen until the bus ride home, and if Benny had been older he would have known that her willingness to have it take place indicated that she was as interested as he was. The teacher wore a proud smile as she relaxed into her seat just behind the driver. A trip perfectly scheduled and executed, and a bus load of quiet children, indicated that she was a good teacher and that she might get a call from Norman, her chance to pose. What was going on behind her was quiet but it hardly would have been the subject of a conservative painting. Many histories were influenced that day and neither the class nor any individual in it was ever the same. There were eleven first kisses, seventeen hugs, and three slight pettings, all unscheduled and all deeply influential. Benny reminisced that there might really be something to scheduling things completely just to find out what would squeeze through the cracks.

His thoughts were interrupted by the sound of Charlene humming in the kitchen. In three months they would celebrate their tenth anniversary. He didn't know it but she was counting the days, well maybe not counting but well aware of the date of their anniversary.

Thirteen years after their first kiss, Benny proposed to Charlene at the art institute, but without the physical presence of the teacher. Now Benny was going to risk it all. All of their good years together were going on the line for his next journey. The only credit you get in this life are on things like credit cards, and all they demand in return for this credit is your continued interest. Come to think of it, interest is exactly what Charlene wanted too. She wanted as much of Benny's interest as she could get, but year after year she had been willing to settle for less and less. Their relationship detoured from the path revealed during their first kiss. Benny considered that his years invested in their relationship gave him credit with Charlene, but as he pondered his next journey he knew they didn't. Relationship is neither rewarding nor interesting when it is attempted on credit or when it must fit into a schedule. His marriage resembled their field trip to the art museum, except that both Benny and Charlene were now being the teacher. They scheduled their time; they knew when they had to be at work and when they needed to be at the mall. For a while they had attempted to schedule their intimacy, but discovered that the same intimacy natural to them as children had disappeared as adults. He loved her, still, and thought she loved him, but there were too many things that needed to get done. With a bit more perspective he would have realized the real problem; he didn't. The real problem was that their lives were too long to pretend intimacy so they substituted meaningless gestures and symbols for natural intimacy. If this was like last year, he would remember his anniversary in the nick of time and support the local florist. She would pretend to be happy with the flowers and, in return, give him something he didn't need to seal a love they both spoke of but no longer felt. Their love was like a third political party, it just didn't get much air time or attention.

Yes, he would undertake the journey, he would throw all caution to the wind. It didn't make sense to do it, but he reached deep within himself and mustered all of his remaining bravery and stood up, leaving the couch far behind as he walked toward the television, leaned over, turned the channel from seven to nine, looked closely at the screen and, satisfied with what he saw, turned slowly, walked back to the couch and sat down.

He couldn't watch the screen; his head was full of ideas. What would people pay for the convenience of being able to change the channel without having to stand up and walk to the TV? He felt a rush of energy within him. He called to Charlene, who obediently came in from the kitchen. He presented his idea to her. The very fact that he had an idea to present to her that had just arrived from nowhere made her look different. She noticed the spark in his eye, she had not seen that spark for years. She loved him and that spark; love experienced is so different from love remembered. She was tired of remembering love and had been longing for this moment. She had not been able to admit that she was tired of remembered love, so all she had been left with for years was being tired. It took no time at all for the spark to burst into flame. Love was theirs again and out of such a short journey on his part.

Fifteen minutes later they climbed out of bed and spent the next several hours inventing together and gathering various items from around the house, the cross context ingredient being first-aid tape. The first television remote control was created! It consisted of a broom stick taped to a ruler. Crude, simple and not very pretty, but Benny could change the station without getting off the sofa. In his instant of discovery, he became far less interested in what was on the screen than in the process of switching channels. In that same moment he became interested in everything. He woke up. One irony from this situation was that while the very idea of his invention invigorated and enlivened him, it also ultimately stopped millions of TV viewers in the future from taking the very journey that appeared to be the source of his awakening. The remote control was not really the source of his awakening, it was just the vehicle and excuse he used to get there. The destination was being alive, and at that point in his life he needed a vehicle to get him there.

Ten years later the couple have riches beyond their

wildest dreams, and still the invitation to awaken at each moment. Over and over during their last ten years, they had slipped into the habit and normalization of waking sleep but the good news is that the times between waking moments were becoming shorter and shorter, and, though he was still considered an inventor, he no longer needed an invention to wake himself up. He found numerous ways to wake up. Mountain climbing worked for a while; a guru did too. Ultimately, a point that few people get to early in their lives, he discovered his ability to awaken by himself. He no longer needed to invent something, climb something, worship something, or even return to his first kiss to awaken himself. The grin on his face moved across his cheeks without apparent muscle movement. From this place there were no more journeys. He didn't need to go anywhere and he could no longer invent. He could create, and that is what he did for the rest of his life and beyond. Created everything and everyone without limitation. He called it a dance—what is possible for each of us.

Television, aside from the stupor it puts you in, also lets you know what you ought to think and what you ought to buy. It gives you a perpetually simplistic view of who is good and who is bad, what is right and what is wrong, what will make you happy and what will make you sad. It presents you with the scripts that you will be at least tempted to play out in your own life. It is difficult sometimes to tell if TV is leading the way, slightly ahead or following right behind you, pushing you on your way. If you get a new Lexus you will be happy. If you get the right peanut butter you will prove that you love those children of yours. There is a purpose to everything you see on the screen. The initial purpose is to get you to watch more TV, the secondary purpose is to have you think in certain ways, and the tertiary purpose is to have you buy products. None of these three purposes are created by you, they are set up and defined by people you will probably never meet. You open yourself up when you enter the trance state in front of that box. Perhaps you should be more careful to whom you open up.

If you quit TV, you will quickly discover that you have more time every day. You are told that there are a limited number of hours in a day, which may be true on one level. But at the level of our perception you have the number of hours you perceive you have, which varies drastically depending on how busy you are. If you have nothing to do for a day, and do nothing, you will quickly discover that a day is very long. If you have a project you are working on and a movie you just must see on TV that evening, your day will be gone before you know it, before you know anything. Time stands still when you are doing nothing; it disappears when you are busy.

How much of your time do you wish to spend sitting behind a box watching colored lights dance without any direct influence from you? Watch people watch TV and you will soon discover what trance looks like. The people who are watching are neither happy or sad, awake or asleep, they are vacant and empty. Try to carry on a conversation with someone watching TV and you will quickly discover what a nuisance you are.

Quit TV cold turkey. By quitting you can win. You will have more time. You will be smarter, you will have fewer images of murder and mayhem in your head. You may even develop your own view of what is happening in the world rather than buying somebody else's. You will probably not be tempted to buy as many things so you will save money and not be let down as often by products not performing the miracles promised. You might even decide that the world is a more wonderful place than TV tells you it is. Without the addiction to the box you could probably spend more time with the people you really care about, rather than the two-dimensional actors on the screen. Perhaps most important of all, you will lower your tolerance for what it takes to entertain you. Your child crawling across the floor or saying a new word can be ignored if there is a particularly high-paced chase scene on the set, but as you wean yourself from the frantic, contrived, and gruesome style of entertainment on the set, you will discover that you can be entertained by the simplest things right around you. You live in a very entertaining world actively waiting for you to notice it.

It took me several years without TV to discover how crazy it is and what an addiction it has become for most people. While I was watching, it seemed harmless enough; it isn't. Like a career, TV feeds on your life, it is insatiable. Like so many other things, the only way to see the effects of it is to quit and then notice, over time, how your life changes. TV is optional; if it is mandatory for you then you are in trouble. Turning the television set off and keeping it off is a big step in reclaiming your life.

5

"Thou Shalt Be Consistent"

I spent hours with my daughter. She was about eight months old. I took her to the park, and then realized that going to the park provided me the opportunity to have time in transit, a goal, a destination other than where I was. A quest to get to the park. A small realization, but how much of people's lives are focused on getting to somewhere other than where they are? I stayed home and played with my daughter. Rather, I watched her, actively. I sat on the floor with her in my arms. I looked at her, gazed at her for hours. I spent time with her, hours. Watching her was tremendously rewarding. Everything in the world was her, to her. Anything she saw and heard and felt she included as part of herself. Not having developed consciousness yet, she was still the whole and thus offered me a doorway to the whole. She had no need to control anything and just existed with nothing added. She was where I had once been but had forgotten. She was not yet alienated, attempting to dig her own fox hole for protection from all that she perceived to be other than herself. She was connected, and I, to some extent, was again becoming connected.

It is difficult to maintain importance while being a full-time mother or father. There is lip service paid to the importance of the family, but that is as far as the external reinforcement goes. In our culture, to say that your career is being a housewife or a parent is to say that you don't have a "real" job. The young child does not have an identity crisis because the young child does not have an identity. Being an adult, which means having developed an identity, provides extended opportunity for identity crisis. My daughter was a threat to everything that was important to me because beyond food, warmth, sleep, personal contact and a diaper change, my daughter needed nothing. Her life was as simple as mine could get, and it constantly pointed out how complicated my life had become. The opportunity to be with a young child provided me with a tool to strip away the layers of the illusion I had built.

If my daughter could not see something then that thing was not there. I constantly believed that all kinds of things existed that I had never seen. I had never been to China, yet I was certain it existed. For my daughter there was no China, no town in which we lived, no next meal; there was only the moment and what she could perceive in that moment. I am not suggesting that this is better than what adults do, but watching her allowed me to begin to discover how much I had added to every experience. She revealed to me some of the assumptions and thoughts I had previously taken for granted. As she grows, she continues to perform this function for me; the more time I spend with her the more it reveals about me.

Though my wife and I had worked together for years, we now began spending "nothing" time together; time doing nothing, when we could explore who we were without having the pressure of getting something done. We had proven we could work well together, play well together, and now the opportunity was to discover if we could do nothing well together. In this process, we discovered that she was addicted to doing things. She would do the dishes in much the same way that I had submerged myself in work. There are a lot of chores around the household that demand completion and threaten to throw the house into chaos if they are not done. My wife compulsively worked around the house, with a narrow focus on the job she was doing at the moment to the exclusion of everything else. Here again, a familiar monster reared his head and said, "When you get this job done, somehow everything will be better." She did the dishes to get them done so she could get to the wash so she would have the time to clean the front room. She built a path of activities she walked on. The activities might vary from day to day, but there were always activities that defined her day. In the absence of a salary or an annual review, she would judge her worth by what she got done. Time doing nothing with our daughter was an extravagance that got in the way of what she had to do. I was in the way of what she had to do. It came as a stunning realization to her that she never just sat doing nothing.

Given that she didn't have what was considered a real job, she could not even justify escaping from employment. She had to keep working all the time. It is little wonder that so many housewives, who have been housewives for years, are in therapy or on some anti-depressant drug. Housewives are entrepreneurs with the most difficult bosses in the world, themselves. They are both slave and master, and they never stop working. Even when they do pretend to relax, they know there is more to do.

It had appeared that I was addicted to work and my wife was unemployed. It became apparent that her addiction to "doing" was deeper, more justified, and more fortified than mine had been. "If I don't do _____, it won't get done." She would fill in the blank often with any number of words. It wasn't the jobs that made her do them, it was her escape from discovering who she was. I suspect that I have just offended many people by the previous line. Stay tuned and give me a chance to explain.

There is a difference between compulsively doing something and just doing something. Compulsively doing something is the result of the importance you put on and derive from your accomplishment. You could get a tremendous amount done in a day and still not lose yourself in the process. The way to perform this magic is by being in the moment as you are doing things. If you think anything will be better or even different when you get a specific task done, then you are caught, hooked, to the task and pulled out from the moment. If you consider that you will be a better person for having completed something, or you seek any attention at all from anyone for having done something, you are again hooked and pulled out from the present and into the future.

My wife thought she was good or at least better if the house was clean. She thought she was better if the wash was done. She wanted me to have a good dinner and an organized house, and she wanted me to appreciate her for having done her activities. The right activities, the good activities. In short, she wanted a pat on the head from me. She wanted to be told she was good by somebody whom she loved and trusted, two attributes she did not have for herself. She would perform her duties, duties she perceived she must do, in the hope of being acknowledged or rewarded by someone other than herself. This is the definition of slavery. Each day she looked a little more like a slave, but neither of us had noticed because we were both too busy to see the obvious.

I have heard that in Zen monasteries there are daily mundane activities one does until one is able to be present in the moment. Raking a garden would be done each day for hours, until the person raking discovered that he or she could both exist and rake at the same time. Activity does not preclude or justify existence. If I had not quit my job, we probably would not have noticed my wife's addiction to her job until it was too late. Slavery was abolished many years ago, but it is still alive, if not well, in many households across America. It is all the more devious since it is not recognized or acknowledged.

My wife began the process of quitting her job. She attempted to wash the dishes when she was washing the dishes. She spent some time each day just sitting, doing nothing and watching, while all she had to do buzzed in her head. I began helping with housework, which took away some of the dreaded responsibility for having a neat house, a house that was not messy like the one she had grown up in. Anything we did became an excuse to be present in the moment, rather than back in the past or more often out in the future.

My mother kept a tidy house and cleaned when I was not at home. My wife's mother kept a pigsty, and hardly ever picked up or cleaned anything. I operated on the principle that houses were normally neat and tidy, while my wife considered their natural state to be chaotic messes that were impossible to neaten. My wife didn't want to be like her mother so she included in her cleaning a message to her mother that she would not follow in her footsteps. One of my wife's prime identities was being "not her mother," mine was being a bread winner, a silent provider like my father had been.

What do you perceive you *must* do? What do you do because you will somehow be good or right if you do it? What do you do because things will be better if it gets done? What do you do that you don't thoroughly and completely enjoy doing? Quit doing anything that you don't love doing. If you don't love doing it, you are not doing a very good job of it anyway. Love is inclusion. If you cannot include what you are doing then you are, at least to some degree, alienated by it, which leads you away from who you are. The farther you get from who you are, the less you know of yourself and the crazier you become. Quit anything you don't love to do. Never, ever, do anything you are not passionately interested and involved in. If you don't love anything then don't do anything.

Your disposition toward what you do is created. It is made up each moment and can change from moment to moment. By watching children, I discovered that one moment they like carrots and the next moment they do not. One moment they can't stand each other and in the next they are best of friends. Everything in their world changes from moment to moment. That is part of the blessing of being a child. As an adult there is a rule which eliminates flexibility. This rule is seldom spoken, it is usually under the surface, supporting lots of other rules that are more superficial and much more obvious. The rule is, "Thou shalt be consistent." There is no consistency in life. Everything changes. Some things appear to be consistent when you compare them to things that change more rapidly. Consistency is relative; thus what you look at defines consistency. You can love cleaning the house one moment and hate it the next and love it the next and hate it the next. This whole time you can be cleaning the house or not cleaning it. In the moments you love cleaning, the quality of cleaning you do will be very different from the moments you hate it. But even more important, the quality of cleaning is your quality of life in the moment.

Work is anything you don't want to do but are justified in doing for some reason or other. Play is anything you don't need justification for doing. In this society we have reversed this order, and we say that your play has to be justified and work is just something that has to be done.

Thus we put the cart before the horse and wonder why the journey is so difficult.

"Thou shalt be consistent." I had to go to work, I had to come home, I had to lose myself in a routine that defined me. The routine took over and I disappeared. Doing the same thing each day at about the same time is consistency. Vary anything from the routine and people get upset. Wrong is anything other than the expectations we have, and the expectations are based on routine. Part of what we love to hate so much about a job is that we at least have some idea of what we will be doing or where we will be. We have to be in a particular location or doing specific things for a period of time each day—consistency. Watching my wife wash the dishes was an exercise in consistency. Glasses first, then plates, then silverware, and then the pots and pans; this is the order that made the most sense, the right order of things, and the very idea that perhaps she could do the plates first upset her. She did the glasses first because they were the cleanest of all the dishes and the water was the cleanest. Certainly, I could understand the logic in that. Anything worth doing is worth doing consistently, and there has to be a reason or a story behind why it is done that particular way. Of course nothing new would be discovered, invented, or created if we all followed this rule, the rule of consistency, but invention is a small price to pay for security. Or is it?

If you doubt your commitment to consistency, your willingness to follow the rule, "Thou shalt be consistent," try not following the rule for a few days. Eat your food with the opposite hand. Talk on the phone using the other ear. Sit at a different place at the table. Take a different route to some place you go often. Shave with the opposite hand. Put on your shirt or blouse inserting the other arm first. If you want some more difficult exercises, try having your voice rise slightly each time you say the word "is," or try gesturing with your hand with each verb. If you really want influence over your life, try exerting influence over the little things. Quit playing by the rule of consistency and you will discover that you wake up in the process.

The rule of consistency has you enter into waking sleep—automaticity, automatically doing things in a certain way, initially because that way of doing them makes sense to you, but then because it is how you have done them before. Consistency is living from the past, bringing the past to the present in order to make the future more predictable and thus less scary. Most people, given the opportunity, would not turn the ship of life around and have their future be identical to their past, but the rule of consistency is the process of doing just that, without the awareness you are doing it. Quit obeying the rule of consistency and you will continually be surprised and living in wonder, in the moment, like a young child.

Stories

Rules

Stories, Rules and Presuppositions

Presuppositions

A game can be defined as making what isn't more important than what is. Any game has rules, that is the nature of a game. While you are playing a game, the most essential element is to obey the rules of the game. Looking at the rules, mentioning them, or considering whether you want to follow the rules interrupts and even threatens the existence of the game. The rules define the game, and prohibit one game from disappearing or blending together with all other games. Rules give games structure and give people structure as well. They let you know where you stand and where you should stand. There are two types of rules: 1) Optional Rules, rules that are made up, and 2) Mandatory Rules, optional rules that you don't yet know are made up. If you do not adhere to an optional rule there will be an optional penalty. You always adhere to a mandatory rule, and you usually think you know what your penalty will be for doing otherwise. Turning optional rules into mandatory rules sets you up as a God opposed to the very universe you live in. There are no mandatory rules. Living life without mandatory rules is a reflection of one's wholeness.

Acting as if something is mandatory when it's optional makes you crazy. You are playing the game of life, you have no choice about that. You will play it as long as anything exists. Even if you die you will still play it, because as long as anything is living or existent the game of life goes on. There are an infinite number of optional games composed of optional rules. Some optional games are played by many people at the same time. The American game is quite popular right now and like any game it is defined by specific rules. To perceive these rules, you must get out of the game and watch it. While you are in a game, you are too busy playing to gain anything but a tiny, narrow perspective on the game.

When I quit Shearson I stepped out of at least part of the game. I exempted myself from one of the main rules, "Thou shalt work," and by doing so set myself apart from the game. I then further distanced myself from the game by questioning many of the rules I had thought were mandatory. Being a radical is revealing mandatory rules as optional, and then exposing the optional rules as being optional. I became a radical, not an outspoken one with a point to prove, those people are still playing the game by resisting the game, but I behaved radically. By degrees, I quit more games.

The American game, which I had always thought was mandatory, revealed itself as optional. I was stunned. With a bigger world view, I might not have been so surprised. People who enter a different culture, and submerge themselves in it, quickly get a view of the American game from the outside. Imagine living within a tribe that lives off the land. Very different rules apply. The whole structure of life is different. All cultures have their own rules. I define a culture as an entity with five or more people who live in proximity and share a set of rules. Five seems to be the magic number. An individual does not create a culture, there is simply the opportunity to do what you will. With two there is the possibility of contradiction or cooperation, but no mediator. Three provides the opportunity to take sides, while four brings things back into balance in a for or against way. Five people together provide variation, an odd number to keep things off balance, a mediator, and enough points of view to have things become confused sufficiently to require consistency in order to get along.

By exiting the American game and going to another culture, you would soon learn and play by the rules of the other culture. This process is acceptable, and there are legal ways of doing so; change your nationality, give up your citizenship, and so on. In other words, if you do so you are exchanging the American game rules for the intercultural rules. What is not "acceptable" is exiting one culture without entering another one.

Within the optional rules there is another division, rules dictated by culture and rules that you determine. Within the rules that culture dictates there is a whole analog of obviousness and seriousness. The degree of penalty for breaking a rule indicates its seriousness, while the degree of questioning a rule reveals its obviousness. There are rules everybody knows and most people follow, and rules almost nobody knows and everybody follows.

In general, you are born into a culture, your parents train you to perceive that culture, and you live and die within that culture. You learn very quickly what you can do, must do, shouldn't do, and can't do. You discover the penalties for breaking rules, and life becomes the process of more or less following the rules, or at least trying not to get caught. You define yourself by what rules you follow and what rules you break. In other words, your relation to the rules becomes all important. Rules become the very air you breathe, and life becomes the game you are born into.

Culture is a game consisting of entirely optional rules, though viewed from within the culture optional rules seldom appear optional. An individual does not need to abide by or belong to any group larger than four people. Larger groups, however, are sometimes difficult to avoid. Working for a company with more than four employees creates a "work culture." There are many groups of more than four people begging for your membership. For example, become a Catholic, join a baseball team or a bowling league, collect stamps, start smoking, quit smoking. When you become a member of a culture, the optional rules appear mandatory since your membership may be jeopardized by breaking a rule.

Rules that you know to be true become facts for you or they disappear. Rules that you doubt become occupations, things to work on or play with. And rules that you don't like become things to resist. The business of life is relating to and playing with rules. "Thou shalt work," is an American game rule, as is, "Thou shalt be consistent." Both of these rules exist in some form in most other cultures as well. You can break any rule that is optional, and breaking that rule without adopting one in its place is the definition of quitting.

There are both hierarchies of rules and hierarchies of games. The structure of all these is complicated enough that billions of people can play within it for God knows how many years and few of the people will ever notice that the whole game is nothing but a pack of cards. Anytime someone obeys or resists a rule, they reinforce not only the rule but also the game that the rule defined as being mandatory. As a culture matures and decays, it increases its number of rules. In the old West, the law was whatever the sheriff said it was. Today it takes hundreds of lawmakers, millions of law enforcers, interpreters, judges, teachers, and criminals, lifetimes to figure out the rules. The rules for the American game have become so complicated that it is a very laborious game. This difficulty helps to masquerade the fact that it always was and still is a game. Playing a game without knowing it is a game creates unhappy, dissatisfied players. People live in a haze, in a maze with life dictated by so many rules that they no longer can tell right from wrong.

One of the rules of the American game is that you must know right from wrong. We are mature enough as a culture that rules conflict all over the place. People are torn apart as they think they are obeying one rule while they discover they are breaking another. People attempt to define their own rules while all of their rules must fall within the games they are playing. The church says one thing while the state says another and yet another. You are supposed to help out your neighbor, but at the same time you are supposed to compete with him or her. You are supposed to love your neighbor, but not make love to your neighbor unless you have a piece of paper that says you are married to him or her. The rules are enough to drive you crazy, and they do.

You are playing in games and following rules and breaking rules that you don't even know exist. For every rule you break and every rule you follow there is a cost. It takes time to evaluate the rules and the costs, just doing so would keep everybody on Earth busy forever, ask a lawyer. Who needs rules? Who needs games? There are rules about who needs them.

Basic philosophical assumptions (presuppositions) underlie every game. One of these primary rules is that you must have rules in order to act well. This statement reveals an internal contradiction, because the very rules that the statement claims the importance of define the outcome, acting well. Underlying the Judeo-Christian American game is another primary rule, presupposition, that left to their own devices people will act badly or at least inconsistently, which passes for badly. The religions that helped form the initial rules of the American game flaunt this presupposition overtly. "You are a sinner," they say. You are born into sin and must strive your whole life to cleanse yourself. Not surprisingly, most religions have a nebulous formula and structure of rules for the very cleansing that you need. This will only cost you ten percent of your income and all of your life to find out. You will, of course, receive a return on your investment but that will be in the life hereafter, something the existence of which is insured in the presuppositions of the religion raising the money.

Any game, given time, will become sufficiently complicated that it will tear the participants apart by contradicting rules. Between games, the confusion and complication becomes ever greater. A football player must stay within the boundaries of the field, and within those boundaries he is encouraged to do extreme damage to another person while being paid well for doing so. He must always seek to do the maximum amount of damage, cripple the other player if possible, while pretending to adhere to the rules of the game. The rulemakers of the game must make the rules loose enough to allow the violence which contributes to public attendance. If too many deaths occur, new rules are made, but injuries that show up as permanent conditions once the athlete is out of the public spotlight are acceptable. Football is more complicated than "Christians and Lions" but the fundamental rules are the same: controlled war waged for an audience. The combatants, of course, are to change their behavior entirely once they step off the field. They are to be nice and gentle with their children and wives. Football is an easy example; examine any game that is presently being waged and you will discover equally ridiculous contradictory and unlivable conditions.

Q

There he was, walking through the woods, when he caught a glimpse of something above the trees. He wasn't sure what it was but knew that it reminded him of something he had seen before. Quickly he went back over his past, searching for anything to make sense of what he had just seen. He settled on a time when he was ten years old and his grandfather had taken him on a trip to New York. He was awakened early, without warning, to be taken to see his grandfather's mistress. He was surprised to be awakened so early, and even more surprised to be hauled off unceremoniously. He searched back over the events of that day to the long silent car ride with his grandfather. The lack of conversation seemed to heighten his sense of sight, and he watched everything with the attentiveness of someone who doesn't know where he is going and is concerned about the safety and outcome of the trip. He recalled that state of heightened awareness and remembered that his grandfather did not share it with him. His grandfather seemed to be in a trance, squeezing little out of the present moment, having put life on hold until they got to their destination. He was nervous, grandfather was so preoccupied it was as if he wasn't there.

Suddenly, through the mist of the early morning, the tops of large buildings rose ahead of them. They were on a bridge entering the largest city he had ever seen. Back then it was the largest city in the world. New York City sprawled ahead of them in all its height and splendor. The image of the top of New York City sticking out of the early morning mist was tied to his present glimpse of the tree-tops. On that memorable day so long ago, his grandfather was taking him to see the Statue of Liberty. His grandfather in his broken English called it the Status of Liberty. His grandfather never lived to see the facelift she went through several years ago. It's a good thing too, he wouldn't have liked it. I suspect grandfather would have thought it appropriate that liberty show some signs of age. After all wasn't she there to show us the status of liberty? Grandfather thought so, and he thought enough of her to make her his mistress.

He was sure he had seen a tall building through the tops of the trees. He walked faster and faster toward what he had seen and was surprised by more and more glimpses. Finally he reached the end of the trees and was treated to a view of NEW YORK CITY in its full splendor. There were the tall buildings, some even taller than he remembered. There was the gigantic city that had grown, like he had, enough so that it still kept him in awe just as it had that early morning with grandfather. He had not seen this city since that morning and was overcome by the beauty and sheer size of it. Although he had not known where his walk would take him, he had certainly not imagined that he was so close to the Big Apple.

He had nothing planned that morning and nowhere particular to be, so he kept walking. Once he reached the outskirts he discovered that the city was very different up close than it had been at a distance. It had looked so clear and clean, unified and whole from a distance. Up close it seemed like infinite fragments with no common denominator, each fragment vying for his attention and making little or no sense in and of itself. He was lost and confused. He was overwhelmed and scared. He was excited. He spent the day wandering the streets. He gathered souvenirs of his trip. He bought a BIG APPLE hat, he got a match book from the Plaza Hotel, a New York Yankees pennant, two hot dogs from a street vendor (those he ate with relish), and he purchased several picture postcards just to prove to himself that he had been there and to remind him of his day in New York City. He had many adventures that day. He had the most exciting and educational day of his life and returned late, via taxi cab, to the edge of his woods. Tired and full of hot dogs, sounds, pictures, and feelings he walked quickly home, curled up in his own bed and went to sleep to dream about his day.

Games split the whole into illusionary separate parts. Presuppositions underlie the basic givens of the game, and rules define what can or cannot, should or should not, be done within the game and the penalties for breaking them. By working together, games, presuppositions, and rules obscure life from us and replace it with a hollow shell that we call life. The best that people can generate within this structure is a hollow happiness based on the emptiness pretending to be fullness. You never had a choice about whether you played the particular games within games that you are involved and trapped in. As you see them, they change from appearing real to revealing themselves as imaginary. You have the ability to examine the games, the presuppositions, and the rules which dance you like a puppet. To get out of the game, you must examine the game. You must reveal it, see it, play with the game itself. In this process you will have an existence separate and distinct from the game. You will discover that this is a friendlier place than you thought, and that there are no mandatory rules.

7

Deer Me

After quitting my job, I waited until the urge to do something left me and I was no longer interested in working. This took several months during which I pondered, to the best of my ability, what I would do if I could do anything I wanted. I learned to perform simple activities without anticipating completion and without using completion to prove my own worthiness. When I had settled into a new routine of doing almost nothing, I quit doing nothing. When it was obvious that I didn't *need* to do anything, I could finally do something. Doing had become irrelevant.

I set a date to lead a workshop teaching people about Neuro-linguistic Programming (NLP), which I had taken extensive training in while I was a broker. I vividly recall that first weekend workshop. I was terrified, and planned enough exercises and wrote enough lecture notes to keep the participants busy for at least a month. My plans were defensive, an attempt to deal with what is reportedly the biggest fear of people in this country, public speaking. My mind was clearly not yet my own, in that I made internal pictures of myself being completely embarrassed in front of people. I explored the technology of fear as I scared myself over and over and used this fear as an excuse to prepare more thoroughly. What I was really afraid of was other people. What would they think? What would they do? Would I be liked and appreciated by them? Looking back, it appears quite funny to have cared so much what other people thought, but at the time it was terrifying. I thought I had handled the impossible by breaking the rule that I had to work, but when a challenge is faced and sur-mounted the next challenge always shows up.

On the Saturday morning of my first workshop, I put on a three-piece suit for the first time since quitting Shearson Lehman Brothers. I didn't feel the least bit com-fortable. My suit used to provide me some shelter, hide me a bit, but now it seemed odd. I was overdressed. The workshop went well; we covered much more than we could have expected, and my nervousness even left occasion-ally. By the end of the weekend I was tired and ready to lead more courses. It was one thing to deal with other people over the phone at Shearson, but quite another to be on display in front of people for two full days.

There are so many rules regarding interactions with other people that it is difficult to know where to start un-tangling the mess. The basic and not so obvious philo-sophical presupposition regarding other people is that they are not you, they are separate, they are different from you—unique. At a superficial level this is true, but if you scratch a bit deeper it is not. Your physical composition is roughly the same as every other person on the planet. With slight variation we all have two eyes, two legs, one nose and a head. We all eat, sleep, and relieve ourselves. With some exceptions, we all walk. We all breathe, think, digest, have blood, lymph, and so on. The primary way in which you are different from other people is that you think different thoughts from anyone else. But because of the assistance of culture and the consistency rule, even your thinking is not so different. You may not be another person, but you are so much like them that you have to look closely, and make quite fine distinctions, to distinguish yourself from another person.

The basic assumption that people are different supports many later rules regarding the interactions between people. It sets up the model of competition. If you are different from someone else, then one of you must be better than the other. This is one of the strategies of the mind to attempt to determine where it stands. Competition is born out of difference, and difference is an inaccurate philosophical presupposition regarding your relationship with other people.

This holistic reasoning could easily be expanded to include other species. Monkeys are not that different from human beings. Neither are horses or flowers. When we start removing the philosophical separations, we find ourselves to be very expansive, everything is us. Individuality is the source of all our fear and competition. What if you quit claiming and fighting for your individuality? That does not mean you would necessarily stop being an individual. This reveals one of your biggest problems in life—that what you are and what you think are not closely related. When we explore philosophical assumptions we are not exploring who you are but rather who you perceive yourself to be and who you can perceive yourself to be.

Imagine what life would be like if your initial assumption was that you were the same as everyone else? Really the same in the same way that your right and left arm are both you, everybody is also you. Competition between people would disappear and cooperation would be the new way of life. You would work with others and ownership would fall by the wayside. Everything would be everybody's. Is it possible that a thought showing up in one person would show up in everyone at the same moment? Perhaps it already does. It could be that the only thing between you and other people is the wall you have constructed to keep yourself separate. You don't fight your leg. What if you never fought your neighbor? What if we are all one body, and anything that touches one of us touches all of us? Anything that influences anyone, influences everyone? Even in a family, the differences between members are accentuated as people strive to prove themselves. What if we operated under the basic philosophical assumption that we are all one? For this to happen you would have to quit believing the presuppositions that result in competition and the illusion of separateness. Change the philosophical assumptions and everything that is built on them will change.

Q

She was in love, of that there was no doubt. Smitten, she stood motionless, her eyes large, dark, round, and a little glossy, staring at the object of her affection.

He was perhaps twenty years older than the Marlboro Man, too old by cultural standards, but she didn't care. He was the most beautiful thing she had ever seen in her brief four years. She knew she had to be careful, knew it deep within her bones, and had been taught to be careful and alert every day of her life. She knew her love was an attempt to cross a line, a line that was best left in place.

It was not with abandon but with the fullest knowledge she ever had that she moved closer to him. She was twenty yards away, now nineteen. The combination of fear and love moved her so deeply she wasn't sure she could stand it. She couldn't smile or speak; this was a love she had no idea how to express. It wasn't sex she wanted; it was closeness, touching, perhaps caressing, which she knew his strong suntanned hands could provide. She had watched him tending his garden for almost a month now, but she had never come this close. To dance with such a man, or to share a row of sweet corn. To find some way to thank him for his years of effort in his garden, the produce from which had supported at least fifty generations before her. This contribution could not go unrewarded for another year, another month, another day or another moment.

He had watched her also from a distance, not his distance but hers. He had pretended not to see her, for her sake, knowing too well that in her world at her tender age he was trouble.

There had been a time, years earlier, when he had thought that age would bring clarity. It did to a small extent, but it also kept opening new doors, new areas where confusion was the password, the open-sesame, the only way in. It angered him a little but amused him a lot. He had been married for forty years to the same woman. He loved her, the companionship was good, the sex still plentiful, long after their bodies had passed the age culture defined for active sexuality. She had passed her child-bearing time by twenty years, but they still had sex at least three times a week. Momentary delight and ecstasy is what they gave birth to, not children anymore.

Though the companionship and sex were good, something was missing. A closeness, a touching beyond words, beyond shared history, and into evolutionary new ground. He didn't know what he wanted, in fact needed, but it came as a shock to him when, two weeks earlier he had thought of his young brown-eyed thing at the peak of enjoyment with his wife. He didn't want to, he tried not to, he fought it with the minimal reserves one has at such a moment, but it was no use.

He had never been unfaithful to his wife, though he had fantasies from time to time. His wife had been unfaithful to him twice. Both times with the same man, and both times during a turbulent time in their relationship many years earlier. Thank goodness she had the presence of mind and fortitude to tell him of her indiscretions, or like a splinter left to fester and infect, her meaningless acts might have gained in significance and robbed them of the many wonderful years they have had since.

But this was different. This wasn't sex, though he wasn't sure of that all the time. This was closeness, a kind of closeness between species that is not possible within species. He wanted to learn things from her he had never conceived of before. He wanted to stand by her side and see the world through her eyes. Surely this sweet young thing lacked the wisdom of his wife, but just as surely she must have her own wisdom. She was young, but he knew she had so much to offer him. He didn't want to speak to her or even share her thoughts—he had enough thoughts of his own. No, he wanted a bit of her lack of intelligence, her simpleness, her moving without thinking, her spontaneity, and her beauty.

He did not want to possess her, he wanted to be her, not to get away from himself, but to be both him and her at the same time. He imagined what it would be like to have all of her charms and his assets as well. This imagining, this wondering gave him more energy, vitality and joy than he thought possible. Biological, evolutionary joy. Pleasure in every cell of his body and extending beyond him, alternately a little beyond him and far beyond him.

She moved closer to him and he, throwing caution and his history to the wind, moved toward her as well. They moved very slowly. She uncertain. He confused. She breathed hard through her nose, wanted to run, to bolt, to get away. She was overwhelmed and needed to be prepared to die if she took one step more. She took it and didn't die. He, too, took another step. He had been attracted to her from a distance, but now, this close, he was afraid and much too excited to think. They were now less than five feet apart. They pulled even closer. If he had thought even one thought, she would have been gone, but he didn't think and remained completely aware. They touched, nose to nose for a moment, and then he stepped sideways next to her touching and embracing her. They joined. He was able to think again, or rather, think anew. Their bodies breathed in unison, and he was slowly becoming aware of thoughts he had never had before because it was not in his nature, but now he was not limited to his nature, he was all of nature. He blended with the meadow, the trees, the sky. She danced with Plato, the city, Beethoven. How long this moment, this special unity, lasted is impossible to tell, but the reverberations continued to move outward like ripples on a newly calm lake. It lasted forever, and she was gone. He stood, free, smiling from his toes.

Later that day he took his deer rifle into town and had the chamber welded shut. He lived happily, and more fully, ever after—and so did she.

If you suffer or have problems, it is due initially to your basic assumptions and how they interact together, and secondarily to how the rules that arise from your basic assumptions interact together and with the initial assumptions. To explore this whole mess is to explore the mess, the whole will remain.

Other people, even friends, are a threat to the world you created. This is why one of the steps to reclaiming your life has to do with eliminating the fear of other people. As long as you are afraid of other people you are afraid of yourself as well. It is not cool to be afraid of yourself, so you have built an untrustworthy and very shaky structure to prove that you are not afraid at all.

A result of fearing other people is that they then hold the key to your quitting the cycle of fear, which engulfs and dictates almost everybody's lives. It is not easy to take this structure apart; it is built tightly and is so interlocked that the mind that put it together wants no part of it coming apart. One way to break down all the barriers between yourself and other people is to quit being who you have always perceived yourself to be.

All human interaction takes place at one of two levels. The first and most prevalent level is that people are all one, this is a mandatory condition of existence. The second level of interaction is that of philosophical assumptions and rules. Given the shallow nature of most of our thinking, people look past the obvious complete and whole connection to everyone and dwell on the way their superficial constructs fit with those of another person. As these constructs relate, you either become more flexible and prevailing or you lose. In the inevitable competition, this will not get you out of the game. The only way to win in relationship is to get back to the presupposition level at which everything and everyone is related. To do this you have to have nothing to hide. You have to reveal to yourself and everyone else your shallowest and deepest presuppositions and rules. The very process of doing so will have you discover what you are not over and over again. You need other people in this process because they provide for you at least the appearance of objectivity, which can free you when you get stuck in the demolition of your illusions. There is nothing like being in front of a group of people for you to be able to see yourself. You see yourself in every other person who is seeing you. You discover that you are independent of who you thought you were. You dive into self-exploration through the eyes of others. Any differences you find between yourself and other people is the result of something you made up, some presupposition or rule you created. You find out about yourself from other people, and about other people from yourself.

This may sound un-American, the suggestion that breaking down boundaries is useful and opening up is the only way to self-discovery. It is. In a system built on differences, similarities are threatening. But when the illusion of difference becomes as important as it has, the result is a superficial level of interaction that precludes cooperation and ends in a profound loneliness with everyone lost and by themselves. This is, of course, not the condition people are in but is the condition most people either perceive themselves to be in or are attempting to escape from perceiving themselves to be in. A word about perception: perception is perception, and reality is reality; perception is not reality. If perception were reality, you would be as miserable as you think you are. You are not.

7 ½

"There is No Such Thing as Truth"

We are bordering on a very difficult and important rule, a primary presupposition that almost every act of thought is based on. That rule is, "There is such a thing as truth," closely followed by the highly competitive statement, "You can know the truth." These statements can open the door to a world of right and wrong. Truth becomes right and good, while false becomes wrong and bad. Once this door is opened in combination with the differences regarding people, there can be good people and bad people. Then quickly follows the rule, "You should be a good person."

In the physical world there is no good and no bad, there is just what happened. But in the world of the mind, order must prevail and further distinctions and categorizations ensue that divide, control and organize. Lines must be drawn so the mind knows what to think. Good and bad have an initial dividing line from which many other lines arise.

What would happen if there was no truth? What would happen if the basic assumption that there is truth were itself neither true nor false? Good and bad would disappear and all competition would cease. You could be constantly entertained all of the time and never fearful. The moment you accept the assumption that something is true then something else must be false. Otherwise, you would have to accept that everything is true and contradiction would drive you rather quickly to abandoning true and false altogether. When you adopt that orphan called true and false, life becomes a true or false test for you. It is good to do better on the test than it is to do worse. You better get busy trying to do good. Soon busy itself becomes good and then your job (since it keeps you busy, out of trouble), becomes good and quitting becomes a remote option. Rules are a derivative of philosophy. So, if the philosophy is crazy, as all philosophies must be, all the rules must be crazy, and you had better quit while you are only this far behind.

Imagine that you are mistakenly put in a nut house (not a good word but it gets the point across). You are sure a mistake has been made, but the food is good and so are the drugs. So you decide to stay for a bit.

One of the ways you pass your time is by playing checkers with another inmate named Chip. Chip doesn't quite understand the game. Throughout the game he eats his checkers; just pops one in his mouth and munches it down. His behavior helps you win, because you want to eliminate his checkers, who cares how. It does seem a bit unfair though, and it does make the next game short on checkers. The problem is that occasionally Chip eats one of your checkers. This makes you livid, and you know it isn't the least bit fair. Your assignment, should you decide to accept it, is to teach Chip not to eat your checkers, ever. Your second assignment is either to encourage him to eat his own checkers more often or not to eat them at all, depending on whether you are more interested in playing a fair game or in winning.

How will you teach Chip not to eat your checkers?

If you are even thinking about how to do your assignment, you're in the right place, this institution suits you. You deserve to be institutionalized. It takes someone crazy to attempt any sort of rational solution, or even an irrational one with a crazy person. Crazy means rational thinking doesn't work, and more.

To engage in any pursuit of solution with a crazy person is crazy. Crazy means that one does not abide by the same rules as most people.

The institution you are in, temporarily, is culture gone crazy. The other inmates are your friends and relations, and checkers is anything you are doing. Welcome, the game has begun.

The way out of the institution is through thought, philosophy, and spirituality. One big problem with the institution is that the longer you are here, the more apt you are to forget that there is anything other than the institution, thus the possibility of leaving disappears. The institution, while not of your own personal making, must be obliterated and left behind by you. The only tool you have to aid in your escape from the institution is thought. Thought got you into the institution and it can get you out. Without thought there is no institution. We have institutionalized craziness, called it sanity, and become both the inmates and the keepers.

To stay in the institution, you must not think your own thoughts or explore too much. You must accept your circumstances and thoughts without questioning much. You must hold on to the institution (illusion) as if it is real. To assure your place, it would be best to pretend you don't and even can't tell what reality is as distinct from thought, or pretend that reality is something it isn't. When one is deprived of the realization of what reality is, one becomes crazy. Thoughts can even become reality, and when they do you enter a world of illusion difficult to exit. Since you have misused thought to get into the institution, it takes a massive reassessment to use thought to get out. It is easier to become good at life in an institution than it is to admit your blunder and leave.

Thought is not reality, neither is perception. Reality is your source and more importantly it is who you are. Reality is your constant source of nourishment and existence. Without it you are nuts. Thought can distract you from reality or it can lead you to reality. Which one it does depends to a large degree on how you perceive thought. The more relevant you consider your thoughts to be, the more danger you are in of being distracted from reality. The farther you get from reality, the more complete your illusion, and the more certain is your place and status in the institution. With enough illusion development you can become the top nut in the institution. Is being the nuttiest something worth attaining?

To a certain extent you get to pick your institution. To become an institution, all something has to do is be around long enough in the hands of humans. The institution needs to be highly thought of, again thought is the key. The human mind, in an attempt to produce consistency, squeezes out the value; when enough value is gone, you have an institution. Then no more thought is required. In fact, thought is counter-productive to the daily business of the institution. Independent thought becomes impossible or threatening, and the institution feeds on the people within it.

The nuttier the person, the more he/she justifies the existence of the institution. Thus the larger the illusionary contribution one makes to the institution, the more apt one is to remain institutionalized.

Thought is the way out of the institution. It opens the door and sets you free. What is important is that thought goes on, not especially what the thoughts are. The way into the institution is by making thoughts appear real. You must then hold onto them, define yourself as your thoughts, and defend them against all comers. That will make you crazy, to have the thoughts be more important than the process of thinking.

You have the key. Thought is the key, it works on either side of the door. It can get you in and it can set you free. How you use it may be up to you, then again it may not be.

All philosophies are crazy because they attempt to force order upon the world by using the mind. They arise from the need to prove that you can figure out things, that the mind really is in control of everything and, extended a bit, that you are really the center of the universe. Without the mind being strapped by consciousness, there is no good and bad, there is only neutral. The universe doesn't care. You have built your own world in an attempt to have it just the way you want it. However, one of the elements in having it just the way you want it is that you want to be able to claim that the world is not the way you want it. You have constructed your own world with some help from your friends, your enemies, and culture. You have fortified some presuppositions and rules and made obvious others; you have defined yourself and then for the most part lived within your definitions. You have determined who you are in the most superficial ways to cover up that you have also determined who you are in the deepest ways. By the basic assumption of true and false, you have set yourself up as a person who must judge the universe. That is your real job, a full-time job, a difficult and impossible job.

8

Kniht Tsuj

From the moment my ship landed on Kniht Tsuj, it was obvious that the planet did not welcome visitors. My ship's indicators picked up temperature variations ranging from boiling hot to intensely cold. These extreme changes, which happened at intermittent intervals with no warning, began shortly after we landed. My crew and I quickly discovered that the force of gravity was present on the planet, but it had a dangerously preferential nature. On Earth, our home planet, gravity was consistent to the point that it had gone unnoticed until relatively recently. When Kniht Tsuj doled out gravity in strong doses, we struggled to keep our bodies from being pulled beneath the planet's surface. During these periods, we were unable to prepare ourselves for the spontaneous and inevitable changes in the gravitational pull. Just like flipping a switch, the planet would release us from the force of gravity and the efforts of our struggle combined with zero gravity would rebound us into the atmosphere. After meandering above Kniht Tsuj for awhile before gravity once again pulled us back down, I ordered everyone to remain tethered to the ship with a rope before leaving for explorations. The effects of random forces of gravity were cruel and exhausting. Gravity would alternately tug on us so hard that we seemed to grow shorter, then on a whim, subside with a jolt that gave us whiplash. Meanwhile, everything native to Kniht Tsuj was treated to consistent gravity indicating that the force of gravity was not only unpredictable but also selective.

As Kniht Tsuj's gravity exerted her intense pressure, it seemed to pull on our thoughts as well as our bodies. Being unsure of the damage that could ensue from resisting such mental weight, I warned my crew to let their thoughts flow, especially when they took on a heaviness far beyond anything that normal thinking merited. After washing torrents of grief, depression, and sadness through our minds, we were suddenly released from gravity's effect as it dropped to zero, leaving our thoughts utterly meaningless. This was a planet of great variation, which aimed, accurately, at keeping visitors off balance.

Kniht Tsuj's unfriendly nature made even the simplest things difficult. I should have mentioned it earlier, but from the moment we landed, my crew and I were plagued by a constant, barely audible noise that seemed to be everywhere on the planet. It was an ongoing conversation in which every plant, animal, rock, cave, creature and non-creature consorted with each other in a low whisper. No matter how hard we strained, we couldn't make out the message. Like meeting someone who speaks only loud enough that you know you are missing something, we could hear just enough to know that we wanted to hear more. The effects of this unending auditory assault were relentless. Apparently the conversation was an invitation for the crew and me to fall into a dream state of sleep which hosted every nightmare, fear and anxiety in the known universe, leaving all of us exhausted and fatigued. Fearing for a few crew members who were affected more than the others, I ordered them into hyperspace capsules to spend their remaining time on the planet in suspension and unaware of the torturous elements. Again we discovered evidence that Kniht Tsuj's unfriendly nature was a subjective one, since the noise had a polite effect on the residents and wreaked havoc on visitors.

Having come from Earth, the crew and I were used to the changes and unpredictability of weather. However, this background was not an adequate preparation for the personal nature of the weather on Kniht Tsuj. The plants seemed to get their water from beneath the planet's surface, which led us to wonder if it ever rained on Kniht Tsuj. I have heard complaints about a cloudy day occasionally, but on Kniht Tsuj where the clouds were the same color as the sky, the complaints were more than minor grievances. Kniht Tsuj's invisible clouds were just big enough to hover above a person's head and, without warning, dump gallons of thick, stinky, brown gunk with the consistency of molasses and the smell of cod liver oil.

Being the victim of such a cloudburst was like sitting beside a person who suddenly leans over and coats you with a massive volume of vomit and stench. Kniht Tsuj's clouds only defiled intruders and their possessions, sparing its own inhabitants. Our equipment suffered much from this cruel and unusual treatment.

As if the unpredictability and personal assault of gravity, temperature, and weather weren't enough to decide that Kniht Tsuj was unfriendly, the light on this planet seemed to be against us, too. It was of a different wave structure than anything we had previously encountered. The light waves were so short that objects seemed closer than they actually were, giving my crew and me the experience of thinking we were somewhere we were not. We would move to avoid bumping into something, then discover that it was still quite a distance away, and we occasionally bumped into objects we thought we had passed moments earlier. This was disconcerting and at times even dangerous. The short light waves created a depth problem which made eating (among other activities) very difficult in that, just when we tried to take a bite of something, we found that it was out of reach or had disappeared behind us. The only technique we discovered to adjust our visual apparatus to the short light waves was to radically cross our eyes, which seemed to move our nose forward as our peripheral vision gained a slightly corrected view of the planet. This took some getting used to, and the initial eye strain resulted in headaches that were indescribable. The effects from freezing and melting temperatures on the food, variable gravity bouncing the food around, and random vile cloudbursts deterred us from simply closing our eyes while eating.

During our brief stay on the planet, the only pleasure for me was the momentary absence of discomfort or pain. Our departure would have been immediate if not for the temporary failure of our equipment having been subjected to the onslaught of hardships. I strongly recommend that you avoid Kniht Tsuj and visit less biased planets. The memory of Earth's neutrality, so friendly compared to the subjectivity on Kniht Tsuj, has silenced any complaints I had about my home planet.

9

Quitting Control

The farther I got from being part of the games (by quitting), the more convoluted, complex and absurd the games looked. People were constantly doing things they didn't really want to do in order to get something they thought they might want to have later. The complexity of the punishment and reward system boggled my mind. Anything that could be justified was acceptable behavior. When the rules are too complicated to follow, it is safest to continually repeat what you have done in the past, because at least you survived the past. Repetition defined as security has resulted in some very deep ruts.

After leading several courses, it was time again to attend one. Each moment we are entirely different in spite of the consistency rule. So the person, me, attending this workshop would be a different person than the one who had attended past workshops.

Attending was so much easier than leading. I smiled and watched the other participants. Did they really come there as a social occasion to keep intact as much of their structure as they possibly could? It seemed so. Did the workshop leader really want to teach and do his best to make certain that nobody learned what he was teaching? The participants, it seemed, needed to prove that what they had done in the past was right, thus there was little for them to learn in the moment. The workshop leader was insecure enough that if anyone learned from him he was immediately threatened by their new-found abilities. It seemed that the participants and leader were well-suited for each other. A group who didn't want to learn while appearing as if it was learning, and a leader who didn't want them to learn but could still appear to be teaching. As a child, physical security is at a minimum; the child needs to be taken care of physically. As an adult, physical security is assured and mental insecurity seems to be at a maximum. A workshop leader who wanted to prove that he was better than the participants made perfect sense from the model of competition in which he was trapped.

I went to learn. I discovered that learning is best done when one sets aside all that has been learned before for what can be discovered in the moment. I made up a game. I had quit enough games that I had plenty of room to make up a new one. This game was simple—the workshop leader was God and I was his humble servant. Whatever he said was the gospel just down from the mountain. I knelt to him, I prayed to him, and I did exactly what he said. Surrender was necessary to play this game. I had to make myself unimportant and him infinitely important. The process of playing this game was disorienting. Who was I? I no longer knew. I learned, adopting everything that was suggested and integrating it into my behavior. Without the need to compare it to all that I had contacted before, I was free to learn. I discovered what it was like to be the workshop leader, because my life was made in the image of this God. He wasn't perfect, far from it, but by collecting all possible data, I was filled with ideas and new behaviors that I could sort out later. The workshop leader could not even be threatened by me, worshipers are flattering to insecure people. In the weeks after the workshop, I slowly sorted through all I had learned, setting aside what was not useful to me and keeping what was. In this God game, I discovered that the worshiper is really more powerful than that which is worshipped. The process of being worshipped is passive, while worshipping is active.

Having discovered my ability to invent games, I was tested on my way home from the workshop. As I rode the ferry, I spoke with a minister who had been in the workshop. He told me that he homeschooled his children. Without hesitation, I said that I did too. Up until this point I had never heard of homeschooling, but instantly knew that it was both what I was doing and what I would continue to do. I was being homeschooled. Looking back on that moment, and the certainty with which I adopted homeschooling, I realize that one of the main elements necessary for making up one's own game is trust. I trusted my response to homeschooling and now, years later, I still live based on the statement that I homeschool my children, I do. Years later, I spoke with the minister and he was no longer homeschooling his kids, but he did have a story about how he was too busy to do so. I suspect that homeschooling was neither his idea nor his game, or he might well still be doing it. Reaction is the element necessary to play a game that already exists. In homeschooling my kids, I was less interested in how other people homeschooled than I was in what optimal homeschooling might be. I created homeschooling for myself.

The God game became integral to my interactions with everyone. Still the only rule was to worship and treat another person like god. It surprised me to discover that the game worked with everyone. If you go into the bakery, treat the person behind the counter as a god. As you interact with your children, treat them like gods. Treat every person you meet as a god. Deal with people as if they are perfect. This does not mean that you are imperfect; it says nothing about you except that you are not needy enough to have to prove anything about how good you are to them. It relieves you of the main practice in competitive relating—determining where you stand in relation to everyone else. Wolves spend little time determining the pecking order of the pack, each member knows where they fit. If they forget, a reminder takes but a moment. People never really know where they stand in the pecking order, and they are threatened if they start to get an inkling because they all want to be on top. The God game secures at least one person's position, the person whom you make a God. They are at the top of the pile. You will be surprised how well people behave, and how wonderful they are, when they don't have to fight for their position. Most of the ugliness in the world is created by people attempting to prove that they are where they are not, and attempting to secure some superior position in relation to others. The God game cannot be played as long as one is still competitive, it contradicts too many of the rules of competition. Try the God game on for size to discover how deeply you play the competitive game.

Worship, it appears, is a very powerful way to extract oneself from much of the trauma created by games, rules, and presuppositions. Worship takes the focus off yourself and places it on something/someone else. The very process of doing this relieves you of all pressure, it sets you free. Worshipping is a game of the moment, each moment you can worship not based on performance or for any reason but worship to worship. Anyone whom you cannot play the God game with probably has underlying assumptions or rules that conflict with yours. It is this conflict that will illustrate to you what assumptions and rules you are living by, as long as you don't have to prove that you are right. The God game is the only model of relating that evades a scene with two crazy people arguing about which one of them is the craziest; two people making their presuppositions or rules more important than they make the other person. The whole root of insecurity is making your presuppositions and rules more important than who you are, or confusing them with who you are. Taking this into relationship results in a loveless battle where the craziest person always wins. Since battle is a game based on craziness, the craziest person will always win.

Anyone you can play the God game with will blossom as you blossom. The mind constantly wants to know where it stands and the God game sidesteps this desire, creating where another stands. The mind discovers where it stands by judging; the God game only requires one judgment, and the same one each time. You don't need to worry about worshiping the wrong person, because worship precludes the whole idea of wrong. When your mind must come up with the right judgment, it is under immense pressure and must work overtime. The more you think the less you observe and the more you attempt to control. The God game allows you a way out, a way to quit this cycle of control that the mind gets its supposed value from.

The God game sets up one person as infinitely good and bad. Infinite is everything. What kind of a person can create a god? A person who is already secure. An essential part of the God game is that the person you are worshiping this moment does not appear perfect to you unless you are playing. It takes only judgment to perceive the imperfect as imperfect; it takes omnipotence to perceive the imperfect as perfect. When you perceive someone or anything as perfect, there is no need to resist, all there is is love, love, love. Love is inclusion. By worshiping another as a god you become a god also; it can't be otherwise. Up until the God game, being a god was not an elected position; now it is and you are the only one who needs to vote. Only the votes of the people who are playing the

God game will be counted. The tally prevails in perfection.

The God game might not be easy for you to play at first. The religions have pretty much got a monopoly on the presuppositions about God. Attempts to play the God game will reveal to you just how deeply rooted is your insecurity, and what a basic role religion plays in the games you were born into. Continue to play the game the best you can and you will empty out many rules.

Quitting the City

Few people ride the subway round and round the city just for the fun of it. The people who take that trip are conductors and engineers who get paid to ride. If you want someone to make the same loop over and over you have to pay them, make the loop sufficiently luxurious, or convince them it is the right loop.

The nature of any game is that it is a process of inclusion and exclusion. The smaller the game, the less that has been included and the more that has been excluded. The bigger the game, the more that has been included and the less that has been excluded. The more you can include, the closer you are to love. Rules serve as a defense against inclusion. If you are able to see the rules as rules, and not as something that determines your behaviors, then finally you will discover, in a flash, that what you were defending all the time was nothing. The defenses were defending the defenses. You really are at nothing all the time. However, within a game, you are unable to perceive this. And anything that comes along that you don't understand is considered a threat to the game, illusion. Since most people associate themselves so thoroughly with their illusion, they defend their illusion as if their survival depended on it. When you spend so much time defending, you miss the love and the discovery of who you are.

One of the wonderful things about quitting is that soon you can quit without ever having played. The short cut to homeschooling provided by my immediate acceptance of it, only later to discover the ramifications of my acceptance, exhibits this. The mind, the greatest gamesperson of all time, wants to explore repercussions first; it wants to know where the cart is going before it gets there. The mind wants to know exactly what will happen before it happens, and thus it misses what is happening around it all the time. This process has people lose the moment in an attempt to control the future.

At my first exposure to the word "homeschooling," I knew it was for me. I didn't need to sort out the rules involved in homeschooling, because I could create homeschooling the way I wanted it to be. If you stick to what works, you can't get too crazy unless you cease to be able to observe results. Most people who are used to playing other people's games would have researched homeschooling to discover all the rules it entailed, as if homeschooling were someone else's game. I knew full well that nobody else was going to step in and live the process of homeschooling for me. I had to set up and define the rules, rules that I could live with and that served my children rather than the history of homeschooling. I, of course, researched the legalities of homeschooling for the state of Wisconsin and made sure to abide by those. I did not want my homeschooling game to be ended by the interference of some technicality due to ignorance. To not play the game, you have to know the rules; and to make up your own game, there are still parameters that you must observe so as not to be oppressed by them.

To discover homeschooling, I started to explore compulsory schooling. What are the rules of the school game, and how well is that game working? What are the presuppositions of the public school game? One of the basic presuppositions is that children must be taught. Another is that somebody must be qualified in certain ways to teach them. Yet another is that there are specific things children should learn and perhaps others they should not. By this point, it became easily apparent why the school system was not working well. The underlying presuppositions that supported the foundation were faulty.

Daily, I watched my daughter learn. She was always learning, she naturally wanted to learn and loved learning. Learning for her was love; it was the inclusion of more and more into who she was. As she learned, her thinking grew larger and larger. She didn't need to be taught, and certainly she was the only possible judge of what she learned. Her technique for judging was not to judge at all. She included everything and used what worked more often than what did not. Controlled learning is not learning at all, it's abuse.

It became apparent that the best teacher, if there needed to be one, would be a person who was able to learn the most in every moment. My daughter was the teacher, and I was learning how to learn from her. In the school system, teachers are already supposed to know everything. They are supposed to teach specific things in specific places at specific times and reward accurate regurgitation. School was a game in which the person who learned to play by the rules was rewarded. It was preparation for future slavery. Slavery is the mindless following of rules and acting in accordance with presuppositions. Learn to follow the rules now, and you will know how to follow the rules later. It seemed that the school system provided me with a model for exactly what I did not want to do with my children or myself. When the presuppositions are faulty and the results are not worthwhile, then there is no point in wasting time looking at the structure of rules that arose from them.

About this time, I found a book about a different kind of school, Summerhill. This school was based on very different presuppositions and its results were incredible. Its students were happy, and exceeded all standards set for school kids. The presuppositions were that children were learners, and that given an opportunity they would eventually choose to learn. The children were considered perfect as they were, and were never required to do anything. They did not even need to attend class if they didn't want to. The teachers became salespeople. They had to make their subjects so interesting that the kids would attend class. Basically the kids were free to do what they wanted within very loose, self-governed guidelines. The children blossomed. They were happy, healthy, and eager to learn. They became not only "able" in specific subjects, but well-rounded human beings. Out of an environment with very few rules came students who knew how to learn. The fewer rules the better. Perhaps, left to our own devices, we would not act as badly as we had always been taught. Perhaps parenting had more to do with getting out of the child's way and learning from him or her, than with forcing the child to conform to games already in place. The first book I read about Summerhill was titled *Summerhill - A Radical Approach to Child Rearing*, by A. S. Neill. If I was going to set up my own homeschooling, it had to be at least radical, otherwise why would I bother.

So we quit culture's school game before we started it. Each day we play, and every day we all learn. When my daughter was five it took her about two minutes to grasp nouns and verbs, addition about three minutes, but division took four or five. Roman numerals took her about a minute to master, and percentages about two minutes. Learning something when you are ready to learn is so easy, and learning by some set time table is so difficult. For a while, my wife and I were afraid that homeschooling wouldn't really work; there is always the opportunity to trust or distrust. Not trusting my daughter to learn would be a mistake that could result in us placing her in the public schools, a system based on distrust. I guess if she could learn to crawl and then to walk, she could learn to read and then to write. Certainly reading was no more complicated than walking. In the process of observing Emily learn, I discovered an inherent learning curve. The first part of the curve is marked by more failure than success, as the child or adult learns from each attempt. Here, it is important to reward the trying rather than the accomplishing. Any intervention or attention is likely to reward failures. As the learner reaches the top of the curve, success overrides failure and attention is appropriate, as much as possible, because it will likely reward success. The first part of the learning curve is passive and more philosophical, while the second part is active and more practical.

One presupposition in our homeschooling is that the child is not better or worse upon learning something, no different at all. The mind quickly turns difference into better or worse so difference is best ignored. The process of learning is, hopefully, a life-long process; the child naturally enjoys learning, and the way to reinforce that natural response is for the parent to constantly learn. When someone is teaching, they are not learning. When someone is learning they are teaching.

A school administrator once asked me what my qualifications were for homeschooling. I said that I loved my daughter. She didn't ask me any more questions; she knew that there was little time in the public classroom for love; there were too many workbooks to get done and just too much to cover (I mean cover).

Many times I accidentally slipped into being the teacher, one who already knows. The moment I did so, homeschooling lost the element of play for both myself and my daughter. It does not surprise me that teachers burn out or are not having any fun after a few years. Taking the role of teacher, a dominant role over my daughter was enough to convert play to work and fun to suffering. Learning need not be a competitive game. Our homeschooling was not.

Taking what I learned from homeschooling, my daughter, and playing the God game in my workshops allowed the participants to excel. They had so much fun they didn't even know they were learning. Though initially I did not know enough to tell the participants to quit, we did suspend rules and cultural norms, which circumvented many presuppositions. During this time, the people became lighter and thrived. The workshops were breaks in the matrix of rules and assumptions that the people were imprisoned by. The courses were not about how to play within the rules, there are an abundance of places to acquire that knowledge, but about how to suspend the rules so that the person could get a view of just how easy life could be. The glow from a workshop would last a few days, but the rules and presuppositions and the games took over once the person was back to life as usual. Games are dependent on their players, players are dependent on the games. Quitting work had revealed to me my dependence on the game. The games do not exist by accident. At least at first, games were well thought out and fear driven. They serve an important purpose, to keep everything as predictable as possible and to eliminate possibilities.

Small numbers of people, brave people, continued to come to workshops, but not enough to pay our bills. I was less afraid of leading workshops and, as the fear decreased, so did the structure of the courses. It became obvious that the structure was for me and not the participants. In my first workshop, I had been the teacher who knew more about my subject matter than anyone else in the room; now, through the contribution of homeschooling, I had become the student who knew less and discovered more. I modeled out learning for the people in the courses as my daughter modeled out learning for me. I had much more to learn about people and about leading workshops. There was a nagging emptiness, something I was missing, failing to see. Some structure I was unaware of was influencing me deeply. I knew that it was time to quit something. Never underestimate a person who is engaged in a game's ability to miss the obvious elements of the game, particularly the fact that it is a game.

After our car was broken into for the fourth time, I realized that it was time to quit the city. If I didn't have to work, I certainly didn't have to be near my work, so why in the world was I still living in the city? The presupposition that all cities are built on is that you need to be in a certain place to do a certain thing. I had vacationed at a small lake in the woods ever since I was a child. Most of my dreams centered around being at that lake. If I could live anywhere I wanted to I would live there, or at least near there. It was time to quit the city. We began packing and within weeks we were living in the woods. Having cut through enough illusion, I did not expect the woods to be better or worse than the city, neither did I place on the woods the burden of being different from the city. I took each moment as it came. Superficially, the woods was different from the city, but I knew well that it didn't matter nearly as much where I lived as what I perceived about where I lived.

11
Games Explained

A move, according to the rules, is supposed to be traumatic, disorienting, and problematic. Ours was none of the three because, like Thomas Berry who travels the world without disorientation, we had a large enough view that we didn't need to consider ourselves displaced. If we, even for a moment, considered that where we were going would be different from where we were, a preference for one or the other would have arisen. This preference would have stolen the moment, made us sad to leave or eager to arrive.

Remember to enjoy the scenery while driving on the evolutionary road, but don't forget to attend to your driving. Where the human race ends up is based on your driving ability, where you go, how long you drive, the way you drive, and your driving record. Really, it is. Every

member of the human race is a driver along the evolutionary road; there are no passengers and no one is just along
for the ride. Each driver's abilities determines the future
of the entire human race. Human beings are not a species
designed to coast. The vast number of drivers does not
reduce the personal responsibility of each individual driver.
Nothing you do while driving is more important than anything else, so it is crucial to maintain awareness, and dangerous to drive while being unaware. Ability is determined by your responses as a driver—responsibility.

While driving you respond to:
    your car (*yourself*),
    your car's needs - gas, oil, air (*your needs - food,
        water, air, health*),
    you as a driver (*your thinking*),
    other cars (*other people*),
    other drivers (*other people's thinking*),
    the road (*cultural demands*),
    the weather and road conditions (*biological demands*),
    and all eventualities.

Noticing a potential problem (observation), having
numerous ways to react to the problem (flexibility), pick-
ing the best solution (thought), and then doing it (behavior) determines your ability as a driver. The better you are
at *observation* the more perceptive you are, and thus the
better equipped you are to avoid potential problems before they become real problems. Confusing *thought* with
observation can be a danger, if you drive around avoiding

or obeying illusion and reacting to imaginary problems as if they were real (the hypochondriac driver).

Without *flexibility,* you respond in the same way regardless of weather and road conditions. Thus your response is based on *thinking* about what you did before rather than on *observation* of the situation NOW. This makes you a predictable, but limited and dangerous, driver.

One of the most important factors in being a good driver is knowing what kind of driver you are. You are the common denominator in all of your driving experiences. So if you know your limitations and your competencies, you can drive according to your ability. If you are a good driver, you will not drive too fast for conditions or so slowly that you become a hazard. To know what kind of a driver you are, you must *know who you are.* While some people think this is a difficult or impossible task, it can be done. The most dangerous drivers are those who skip over this step, often thinking that they already know who they are. When you lack the knowledge of who you are, you act out other people's interests rather than your own. These drivers answer to *culture* instead of *themselves* and as such, they define the status quo. Knowing who you are is the first step toward becoming aware of your driving and taking responsibility for your actions. As more drivers either know who they are or pursue who they are, there will be fewer accidents on the evolutionary road.

Your driving constantly influences your driving record and every other driver on the evolutionary road (including future drivers). The test of good driving is not whether you can walk away or crawl away from an accident. It is whether you learn enough from each accident that you and everyone else can avoid similar accidents from NOW on.

One moment we were in the city, and five hours later we were in the woods. We temporarily moved into the cottage on the small lake where I had vacationed for years. At one and a half, my daughter hardly noticed the move, given that she was not dependent on place as much as she cared about the people she was with. She was happy almost all the time. We attended to what she needed: food, rest, diaper changes, and closeness. She provided the rest. Constantly entertained and entertaining, she was a source of lightness.

As I looked around, I marveled at the rules I had been taught about the lake and the house: what was and what was not acceptable behavior, what I must do and what I must not do. My grandfather had taught me that fishing is a quiet adventure. To fish is to row around the lake as slowly as possible, dragging a big dare devil at the end of an old casting rod with lots of line out. Not surprisingly, my daughter was not interested in fishing; she was not even allowed to go, because she would break the mandatory silence. Over the years, I had seen people fishing with spinning rods, with boats with motors on them, talking as they fished, eating as they fished, and all other permutations on the "right" way of fishing. I quit the game called fishing. At least, the game as I had learned it. I made up a new game called fishing, which had few rules other than those that ensured the safety of the people aboard the boat. The old rules were stubborn. I was tempted to long for the quiet, solitude, and certainty of the old order of fishing.

Tradition offered me a way out of the present. I could yearn for what was and miss what is. I declined the offer. I preferred time with my daughter to the old rules about fishing. The whole family went fishing. It was sometimes a raucous affair, and we caught at least as many fish as my grandfather and I had.

I had brought my computer from the city to the woods. It looked a bit out of place at the cottage. I decided it was time to write a book. I sat at the computer for hours, writing. If only my high school or college teachers could have seen me. I was not the kind of student they ever would have predicted would be an author. As a student, I had been a poor reader and uninterested in education. Here I was, writing a book. My first book was nearly a hundred pages long. It was difficult to write. I agonized over my words, I struggled with exactly what I wanted to say and how to say it. I was attached to the book, it was a part of me. I would be judged by its quality, if I was lucky. And if I was lucky, a lot of people would read it, but that was unlucky as well, since I thought the book was a part of me. Looking back, I should have known enough to quit writing, but I didn't. As the manuscript neared completion, I threw it away. It was garbage. I erased it from the hard disk of my computer and quit writing. I didn't consider this to be a failure. Rather, it was a clearing out of some garbage to get to what I really had to say. Within weeks, it was time to write. Writing was effortless and fun. Time flew as I wrote, and I learned from my own writing. It was no longer my book, not a part of me; it was *the* book, words on paper, words that took a certain order of their own, with no control or necessity of my own. Following the "write when it is time to write" formula took patience and, initially, was a slow way to write a book. It was only occasionally time for me to write. The two hundred pages of the book took about four years, from meager beginnings to finished bound book in hand. As we sold the first few copies, I worried about how the book would be received, but soon I let my worries go. Then, like a grown child, I let go of the book as well. People will always think what they think, they will never think what they don't think. Most people would read the book from within their own framework of rules and assumptions, and take what fit while not even noticing what didn't. A few people would read the book in a learning mode, taking each word as the gospel; these few would learn much from the book, and what they learned I could not possibly control.

While the book was in process, my daughter was learning, and my wife and I were trying to keep up with her as we moved from the lake cottage to a house we purchased about fifteen miles away. We had lived in the cottage for a year, an amazing year of play and free time. I led occasional workshops throughout the year, one of them at the cottage. The deer came and ate our discarded kitchen scraps, standing fearlessly within five feet of our bedroom window; they were our neighbors. I recall walking the mile to the mailbox during the winter, and walking back on the frozen lake. A snow storm was in progress, and I lay down on the lake and watched and listened to the first thunder and lightning snow storm I had ever witnessed.

There was no transition from the city to the country. There is a background of busyness, of noise and distraction in the city. Since we had not let this get in our way while we were there, we did not miss using it as an excuse for anything when we came to the country. I have recently watched people move from the city to the country, while thinking that now things will be better. It is a crushing blow to discover that things are no different. People bring the same internal turmoil to the country that they had in the city, but in the city they could easily blame outside influences for it. There is little relief in blaming a deer for one's craziness. If you are deeply immersed in unrewarding, conflicting games in the city, these will probably become more obvious to you in the country.

You can always quit right where you are, because that is where you are. If you think that quitting will be easier at some point in the future, you put yourself in the position of a dieter who will start the diet tomorrow. To quit something is to view it as optional with no preference, personal or cultural, in its continuance or disposition. To quit something is to move from being attached to something to being in the present where all judgments subside. To withdraw support from all illusion, stand back and watch it collapse under its own weight. All difficulties in life are caused when one game clashes with another, or when the illusionary nature of games reveals itself as the rules or presuppositions bump up against reality. Quitting breaks up illusion and begins to reveal reality. It releases you from who you thought you were to discovering who you really are. The whole process of playing any game, living out of presuppositions and according to rules, robs you of the flow of energy. It restricts what you can do and, more basically, what you can perceive. It is an attempt to prove your existence in a specific location in accord with the game. The game doesn't ever prove anything about who you really are, but it gives you a kind of image, a symbol that you can think you are, or fear that you might really be (a Scotty dog or top hat or...). Symbols are two-dimensional and empty; they are representations. To stand for something is considered good in our culture, but to stand for something is also to represent something, to be attached to the thing that is being represented, and thus to associate with that thing so intimately that one becomes a hollow representation. Appearance becomes all important within a game, and, in the game, rules determine perception. Thus, how you look matters, but how you see is controlled. This is a spiral that closes in on itself, and is the very essence of a game.

There is nothing difficult or problematic unless you make it so. Moving is tough if you consider that your present location defines who you are. Moving and quitting are not the same though. With quitting, the game disappears; with moving, you take the game with you. Change is only a threat to the game, quitting has nothing to do with change. Change is only a problem if your perceptions are limited, because change alters your perceptions. Games must constantly adapt to change while appearing not to do so. One of the rules in the American game will illustrate my point: "Thou shalt look young and healthy, and never grow old." It isn't good to grow old, according to this rule. Think about growing old, go to homes for old people and talk with them, explore growing old, and you will discover that it is something that the American game frowns on. The very fact that it is considered bad to grow old necessitated the hiding of old people from the masses. There are cultures in which maturity, age, is considered a virtue, where the older you are the more respect you receive and the better your life gets. Perspective can increase or decrease with age, and the very rule that growing old is bad influences our thinking about old people. What is good about growing old? In a society hell bent on work, the old person has little to offer but a body that needs to be taken care of and supported. An old person is no longer useful. The game of retirement at any age in the American game has one view oneself as worthless.

There are repercussions to any game. Remember, a game makes something that isn't more important than what is. If youth is more important than old age, then you wouldn't even want to see old people, let alone appreciate and learn from them. Many old people are forced into quitting by the very nature of the game; they can't play anymore so they don't play. Being forced to quit is not the same as optional quitting. The rules of the American game force the old people out of the work game that they have struggled to play their whole life. You too will receive the same reward some day. Passive old people submit and quit, while more active seniors resist and become bitter or eccentric. Being forced out of a game usually results in a reaction, while optional quitting does not. Being forced out, or perceiving that one was, is mandatory quitting.

When something is worthless, you throw it away. In the American game, old people are in the way; something to support and keep out of view. I read somewhere that a culture is judged finally on how it treats its older citizens. We flunked. At the same time that we herd the old people out of our sight, we don't look at the kids either. If you arrived from another planet to explore Earth on any weekday, and walked around any town or city, you would conclude that there are no children, only adults in this culture. Children are not yet useful to a culture whose basic rule is, "Thou shalt work," so they, like the seniors, are herded off to specific locations until they are old enough to work. They are prepared for work. They practice going to one location and doing things that they don't want to do for many hours every day, with someone looking over their shoulder and constantly critiquing their thinking and behaviors. That certainly sounds a lot like preparation for work. The young children are taught about being judged and about structure; the old folks have already been judged as "old" and have passed through the structure. You probably don't even know that you will grow old some day. I mean, you know it as an idea, but you don't really know it. If you did, then your willingness to have a future so bleak would fade, and you might even change the game, if not quit.

Games develop lives of their own. We again cross the fine line between whether the game needs the people or the people need the game. The only casualties in games are the players, and the players are always human beings. You will not survive your games. The only question is, will you continue to play them given that they rob you of life? Life is the opportunity to walk freely anywhere you choose, doing anything, and perceiving anything. The iron maiden that the presuppositions and rules of games offer is not life, it is structure. Life is function, games are structure. Life is process, games are stuff, not stuff of life as you are taught, just stuff. Games are not necessary; the moment, now, precludes them. Look around you and you will see the walking wounded, you will see the players on the disability list. You will see the people whose rules confounded them, tripped them up once too often. You will see people trying not to grow old, and spending little or no time with their children. You will see people unhappy, or attempting to appear happy in a crazy world that they never chose and don't know how to escape from. There is no way to win within a game, though you are taught that playing is winning. The games go on, with or without you, and you become a casualty; that is what happens when the games themselves, the rules, become more important than the people ruled. You can think you are exempt, but if you suffer or struggle even the least little bit you are caught.

People go to therapy, take drugs or alcohol to deal with their pain, their past, or the fears of their future. People, are dying in unsustainable games with mock enemies that are supposedly responsible for our traumas. The only way to win is to quit. Quit now. Now is the only time you can possibly quit.

12

Quit What?

How easy is it to quit? It took me many months to quit my job, and even longer to determine that I would never again have a job. For years, the nightmares persisted. Quitting is the one thing that is not allowed. "Don't be a quitter." "Quitters never win and winners never quit." You will be taunted as you even consider quitting. You will argue within yourself. There are millions of reasons for not quitting, and if you look at those you probably won't quit. If you look at the reasons for quitting, you will begin the quitting process, but you will burden it with the idea that you will not quit until it makes sense to quit. If you have to wait to quit, then you are engaged in change, not quitting.

Let's take a small example to illustrate how difficult quitting is. Do you prefer one day of the week over another? Is Monday better than Tuesday, is Saturday better than both of them put together? Remember, it is a game if something is more important than something else. If you were on a deserted island for long enough, days of the week would cease to exist, light and dark would be more relevant to you than what day it was. A certain sign of a game is that if conditions changed, would what is relevant to you change? To people outside the "Thou shalt work" rule, whether it is Monday or Sunday makes little difference. The days of the week are made up, they are an element in a game. There is the work week and the weekend. Does this structure of days being different, which soon leads to preference for certain days, help you at all? It gets in the way of doing what you want when you want. It stops you from working when you might be most productive, and gets you working when you are supposed to be working. It has you and the kids be occupied at the same time. So, in that it is convenient. Otherwise, the kids might get in the way of your work. The work week defines your life, it rules you. It structures every day, and if you don't want to play within the structure you have to get sick to avoid it.

Certainly, this work week structure is changing. More people are now working at home, and some people are working flexible hours, but remember that changing a game is not the same as quitting it. To quit the work week structure is not easy. You have to retrain your body, games take on a cellular existence. They work at such a small level, influencing everything people do. It took me years to realize that I could write just as well on a weekend as I could on a weekday.

What about holidays? Your birthday is different from any other day, isn't it? What about the birthday of Jesus? There are more suicides around Christmas than any other time of year; 'tis the season to be jolly, fa la la la la. When a rule is obeyed often enough, we get a ritual. Birthdays are supposed to be special days. Days that mark your growing older are supposed to be a celebration in a culture which doesn't like old people? Birthdays are supposed to be exciting when you are a child, because they indicate that soon you will be old enough to be worthwhile. They are to be celebrated but disliked when you are middle-aged, because you are not yet unproductive but one more step on the way there. They are to be celebrated in a hollow empty way when you are old, because they indicate that you have survived the trauma for one more year. Aren't old people, really old people, embarrassing?

The whole idea of a birthday is that one day is more important than another. Do you need an excuse to celebrate? If you need a reason to celebrate, then you are celebrating reason. Why is your birthday more important than the day after your birthday, or the day before? It is no different and you know it, but I bet you can't quit treating it differently. For most people, birthdays, as a child, were supposed to be exciting, wonderful events, but they were not. They were days when you ate more sugar than was healthy for you, and on which big people gave you presents that you were supposed to be excited about in certain ways, and small people learned about sacrifice as they gave you presents that they would rather have kept for themselves.

Birthdays probably were celebrated long before you knew it was your birthday.

There is little Johnny. His mother doesn't usually let him eat sweets, but on this day, his first birthday, he gags on a cake from the bakery, and then a big bowl of ice cream. All the grown-ups are around for a change, and they are singing loudly. What a bizarre day a birthday is for an innocent one-year-old. Lest you think that the celebration is for the child, it is obviously for the adult. A kind of pathetic coming of age. Without the structure of a culture, and the games within it, there would be celebration every day. The sunrise would be a celebration as the dark ended and the light began. Each variation throughout the day would be an opportunity to notice something outside oneself and thus celebrate the change. There would be a grumble in the stomach a few hours after rising, which would indicate that the stomach was ready for food. The clock doesn't know when you are ready to eat, only you do, and chances are you have forgotten how to notice. Imagine eating when you are hungry, not when you are supposed to eat. "Hurry up and eat, the school bus will be here any minute. If you eat your toast, then you can have a doughnut. Here is your lunch, get going." Eating could be fun, entertaining and respectful, but it is seldom any of these. It is in the way of production, and anything that is in the way of production is secondary. People who skip their lunch hours, to work even more hours, are certainly better than those who don't.

For your birthday you get a cake, ice cream, and presents but for His birthday, long after he is dead, Jesus gets a tree, worship services, the best retail sales of the year, people singing hundreds of songs to him, and the sacrifice of a day's labor. Jesus must be more important than you are. Of course he is. After all he is the reason for the season. It is blasphemous to question the obvious importance of Christmas over all the other days of the year. If you want to find out how addicted people are to their games, and to the rules the games entail, try not celebrating Christmas without a good reason for doing so, such as being Jewish. To ignore the holidays is to turn away from one of the most popular games of the year. On Christmas, you have to give presents to people you would not even give the time of day to the rest of the year. Dickens said it best: if you don't celebrate Christmas you are a scrooge, and even the ghosts will be against you. Do you really enjoy Christmas? At first your answer will probably be "yes," but look more closely, observe the consequences of the Christmas game. Look at all the pretenses that it reinforces. Certainly, I can't be suggesting that you quit Christmas.

If you could do anything that you wanted on a specific day, what would you do? The idea of having a day to do what you want, anything at all, is threatening to people. You probably wouldn't come up with an evergreen tree in the front room with lights on it and presents under it. Christmas is to be celebrated because it is a more structured, intense game than the usual games you play. The more structured it is, the less apt you are to quit it, and the more costly it is to keep playing. Christmas gives people an excuse to exhibit a craziness that they would not exhibit the rest of the year. It gives them an excuse to get together with family members and watch football on television.

I ask you again, what would you do if you could do anything you wanted on one day? I mean anything. If you had a day without rules, without presuppositions, a day in which you make up the game entirely. A day on which money doesn't enforce rules on you, and neither does work. Who would you spend the day with and what would you do?

Think about it, think more, think hard. Get out of the constraints that you are used to. If you could have any human being you wanted with you on your special day, who would you have attend? If you could have sex with anyone you wanted to on that special day, who would you have sex with? If you could have any food you wanted, what food would you have? What would your day look like? We are taught our limitations so well that it is hard to think outside of them. Would you spend the day with Naomi Campbell, Richard Gere, Benjamin Franklin, or Jesus? Include in your day the fact that nobody will ever find out what you do on your day. Does that change what you would do and with whom? Now extend your day to two days, and discover what changes you might make to your schedule. From two days, extend it to a month, and then to a year. I suspect that by the time you get to a year you start including a bunch of structure; time necessitates rules because it includes repetition. A whole year to do whatever you wanted is much more difficult to deal with than is one day. Quitting provides you with only days when you can do whatever you want to do; most people can't handle this, the very idea of it is too scary.

One realization that comes soon after quitting is that it is only within the game that you want to break the rules of the game. Prohibition increased the interest in alcohol consumption. Diets direct one's attention to food. Rules keep you occupied with following them, while thinking that life would somehow be better if only you could break them for a little bit. If there were no rules, you would not behave at all like it appears that you would while you are living in a world with rules, considering no rules. Rules define your priorities, they determine what you will do, won't do, and should do and, not so obviously, they also completely define what you are able to want to do. When you are in a box created by assumptions, and sustained by rules, you cannot think outside of this box, and what you think you want is determined by the box. What you think you want has nothing to do with what you really want. Thus it appears that without rules people would act badly. If there were no rules people would act perfectly. Within a system of rules, people appear to be bad without the rules and long to break them. We never said "no" to my daughter until she was four years old. Consequently she never did anything we needed to say "no" to.

It is the rules of the game that induce people to break the rules. It is the game that needs "bad" people to make the game important. Rules are lines drawn that one must not cross, but by the nature of human beings, if they are told not to cross a line, some of them will. If they are told not to eat the apple, some of them will. People are perfect, it is just within the games that they seem not to be. From within the game, life without rules looks like chaos; in fact, the games themselves produce chaos as something they can offer a refuge from. Quitting is the only way you can win a game, because as long as you are in a game the game goes on. The game ends when you quit. The game is dependent on you more than you are dependent on the game, hopefully.

It is often the least important games that are the most difficult to quit. Try quitting the holiday game, or the game that makes one day more important than another, and you will discover that it isn't easy. But you can quit.

13
Look for the Signs

There had been warnings. I was sitting at the Steak and Brew long before I quit my job and left the city. My wife and I, and another couple, were sitting at the bar waiting for a table to clear. We are all waiters. All it takes to become a waiter is to think that there is somewhere to get to other than where you are now. Suddenly, I was out of the games. There were no rules for me, or presuppositions either. A physical sensation accompanied this experience, a lightness and strength from head to toe. I could not speak, I did not need to speak. I was glimpsing heaven. Everything was perfect around me. An explanation, which won't do the experience justice, is that energy was flowing through me at such a speed that I could not slow it down at all. In electrical terms, I was a conductor rather than a resistor. This state lasted for several minutes, and went unnoticed by everyone but my wife and me. Neither of us knew what to make of it, thank goodness, because there was nothing to make of it. The state that I was in for that few minutes is the one that now, years later, I live in. In one domain, it is comparable to being in the dark for a few days and then entering the light. It is the difference between being asleep and awake.

There had been other glimpses, but for most of them I had been in situations where I could attribute the lightness to the circumstances. Floating down a white water stream, for example, had produced a similar experience. In the face of the stream, everything that I perceived myself to be disappeared. I, in essence, quit all of the games and was in the moment. Tragedy sometimes does this for people. The car falls off the jack onto a child, and the parent lifts the car. In the moment, magic is possible, even persistent. Outside the moment, one must work hard to have anything "right" happen. Some people call such moments peak experiences, and they can look like peaks from down in the valley, but they are more like just-having-dug-yourself-out experiences; however, that doesn't sound as flowery, and it puts the responsibility for the mess you are in right where it belongs.

Q

Imagine stepping inside an eclectic theater with a multi-dimensional holographic screen, a wave induction sound studio, and the ability to convey tastes, smells, and total body physical sensations. As you enter the theater, the movie starts and you realize you don't know what is playing. You discover that this is not just a movie theater but a playground for an interactive game in which your responses influence the film, frame by frame. The exact influences your responses have on the movie are not obvious or predictable. However, it is certain that your responses are constantly noted and figured in to bias what happens next on the screen. You may decide that your influence doesn't count, or that you have complete control over the entire movie. Neither is the case. The theater's ability to constantly include your responses in a computation that quickly determines what will happen next in the movie is too subtle and too consistent for you to detect or control directly with consciousness. You astutely observe a Catch 22. While your behaviors are being constantly noted and figured in to influence the film, the film is simultaneously dictating your behaviors. It does so by noticing your initial preferences before you do.

The movie continues and ranges from comedy to drama, from adventure to documentary, and from horror to romance. At times, it is so intense that you forget you are in the theater, and you identify so thoroughly with the interactive playground that you and the film seem to be one. Some moments portray a struggle that seems so real you find yourself in agony, as if the difficulties being acted out are your own. The movie keeps on going, and you keep on having responses. You become angry, sad, ecstatic. You get distracted, fidget, and then fall asleep. You become bored and consider leaving the theater. All of your responses are figured in and influence what happens next.

At this eclectic theater where your behaviors influence the show, you have a tendency to turn to superstition or reason (consistent superstition) for answers or solace. For instance, if you move your right foot, and something *nice* happens in the movie, it could be a coincidence. If you move your right foot again, and notice that something else *nice* happens on the screen, you now have the beginning of a pattern. There may be a correlation between moving your right foot and something *nice* happening, and there may not. Since you like the movie better when *nice* things happen, you decide there is a connection. If you move your right foot, and something *nice* happens often enough, you will call it a fact and, since facts are often considered sacred, you will only notice things that prove the fact, as you move your right foot more often. If you move your foot, and something *terrible* happens, you may overlook it and see something *nice* instead. Your discovery of the influence, or supposed influence, that the movement of your foot has over *nice* things happening becomes so important to you that it overrides what you see on the screen. Thus, you watch the movie based on what you decide you see, rather than what is there. This is an initial step in the building of an illusion. The preference for *nice,* and the cause and effect between foot movement and *nice,* have become more important than what is happening in the movie. The theater notes this and acts accordingly (what accordingly means is up to the movie, not up to you). You systematically lose the ability to see more and more of the movie as you construct preferences and then causes and effects to support those preferences. Before long, the movie on the screen is only a distraction from the illusion you have built in your head.

In addition to the movie distracting you from your illusion, there are also many other people in the theater with you, each one of them behaving in a similar but different fashion from you. The other people's behaviors are influencing the movie also as they construct preferences and causes and effects that inhibit their view of the screen. What you and the other movie attendees think and say about the movie is also noted and computed. The sum of interactions among people, and between each person and the screen, is too complicated to grasp, but it seems to be important. Someone in the third row is moving his right foot, thinking it makes the movie more *pleasing*, while someone in the fifth row is trying not to move her left arm because, each time she does so, something *terrible* happens on the screen. At the same moment, a young boy at the back of the theater is nodding his head, thinking that is the way he had something *terrible* happen last time. Coincidence, confusion, and accident rule the day, dressed up as predictability, understanding, and intent. Preferences lead the way in the dominance of flesh over substance as moviegoers seek to control the movie. Competition for control comes with the idea that control is possible. Cooperation comes later as the movie goers realize that they do not directly control anything but their own illusions.

Context, in which you have such an experience, can get in the way of having more. If you have such an experience while you are climbing a mountain, you might then need to find a higher mountain to climb to experience it again. Pretty soon, so much of your time is spent planning the next expedition, you miss the obvious fact that living in the moment, on the peak, is where you always are but don't notice that you are. Anything worth doing can be done from right where you are. There is nowhere to get to.

Quitting will often provide you with a moment of elation; so will a real threat, as opposed to the constant theoretical threat that most people live with. The whole structure of games, with their presuppositions and rules, inhibits peak experiences and deep valley experiences as well. It eliminates the highs and the lows while supporting the middle. Quitting can give you highs, but it may well give you lows also. The lows are residual effects of still thinking that quitting is loss. Once you understand fully that quitting is quitting, the lows will completely disappear. It is the threat of the lows that motivates the creation of the game; not so obvious, it is also the threat of the highs. From within the world of games, neither the highs nor the lows are stable or sustainable, so they are not consistent enough to obey the rule of consistency.

What is going on in your life right now that is revealing your future and where you are heading? One way to observe games and expose them for what they are is to extend them out sufficiently and discover whether you are interested in their end results. You need to allow your personal relevance to disappear and let yourself be worthless. To do otherwise is to attempt to prove something within the illusion. If you discovered that your entire life, up until now, was illusion, what would you do? Would you quit the world of illusion or keep playing? Would you settle for occasional peak experiences and dig in somewhere part way up the mountain? Would you keep climbing, hoping that some day you will really win?

People don't want to win; they don't want to lose either. They just want to play the game. Part of playing the game is pretending to want to win, thus people pretend they want to win. When people are playing the game they are distracted, busy, and best of all they think they know where they stand. They know who they are by the position they hold in the game. Above all, the game allows people to define themselves, separate themselves from the masses, and separate themselves from the void by being something in particular.

Whatever the best moment in your life has been shows you the worst possible life you could have if you were to quit the game. Within the illusion, within games, everything is reversed, or at least out of kilter. Think of the best moment of your life, when you were the most God-like, however you define that. What if that was a valley instead of a peak, and you moved up from there? It isn't easy to have a wonderful life; nobody wants you to. Remember the kid in class who was so much smarter than everybody else that he or she threw off the bell curve, in effect, making everyone else appear dumb? That person is never well-liked in a world of competition. You have to get out of competition, exit the game, and then the smarter or more wonderful you are, it reflects well on you. It is by comparison that you suffer as you look at people who appear better off than you are, and it is by comparison that you alleviate your suffering by looking at people who are worse off than you are. It is by comparison that you know who you are at all. The very idea of comparison gives rise to difference, which leads to good and bad, which has you suffer. Quit the game and you win; you can't help but win. You lose too, because you are big enough to include and thrive on both. Win and lose are the same once you have quit.

14

Building an Identity

I had pretty much escaped the loop. Though I had quit many games, deeper games continued to reveal themselves. Looking at the culture from outside, it made no sense. People looked nuts. Was I being too judgmental? What is a nut? A nut is a soft tender sweet little meat surrounded by a hard protective shell. People were nuts, they are nuts. The protective shell is the game, woven together to protect the sweet tender caring person inside.

It had been six years since I had quit watching television, but I still listened to the radio occasionally. Wisconsin Public Radio is primarily talk radio, hosting people of supposedly different persuasions who invite other people to call in and argue for their points of view. One of the basic rules is, "Your point of view matters," with a basic underlying assumption that you are your point of view.

Another rule is, "You must have a point of view," hiding the assumption that you are bad if you don't have a point of view.

The longer I was out of the cultural game, the more ridiculous the arguments looked. People still argued about whether they were democrats or republicans. The difference between the two had been very clear to me in high school but disappeared for me now. Neither of the parties could be trusted, and either would say anything they thought might get themselves elected. Was there really a difference between the two that made any difference at all? Did people who called themselves democrats have better lives in any way than republicans? It didn't seem so. Was a sports team from Chicago really any different from a New York team? People keep striving to make something different enough from something else that they can take sides and then prove they are on the right side. They fail to notice that the team from New York has traded for several players who used to be on the Chicago team, thus the difference between the two teams is reduced, and yet their allegiance to one or the other remains. People define themselves by their particular persuasion, and who they really are disappears as what they stand for becomes all important.

How would you describe yourself? In what order would you place the adjectives to best let someone know your priorities? Who are you? The process of building an identity (determining who you are) is additive, while the process of observing subtracts. As you look at yourself to really determine who you are, you strip away what has been added (who you have to be) to discover your essence. Do you have to be a democrat or republican? Could you be either? Could you be both? Does it really make any important difference to you which one you are? If you found out that you had one week to live, how much of that week would be spent proving the rightness or wrongness of your political persuasion? Politics is an empty game whose sole function is to divide people and have them appear different from each other. At its base it keeps people occupied, busy with things that don't matter.

What does matter? Why would you do something instead of something else? How do you decide to do anything? If you have to do the "right" thing, then by some criteria, criteria of the game itself, you have to determine what is right and then do that. Doing the right thing has you become the pawn in the game; it is the rightness or wrongness of whatever it is, not you, that determines whether or not you do it.

My daughter, at about three, continually pushed me farther away from the automated, assumed world of games. She didn't want a Teenage Mutant Ninja Turtle, though many kids in the country, it seemed, couldn't live without them. The idea of wanting the little pieces of plastic seemed so ludicrous. My daughter could play with anything, she didn't need the contrived nature of common acceptance or cultural approval.

My wife and I had heard of the "terrible two's." However, we quickly ascertained that, outside of the culture, there are no "terrible two's." My daughter began forming her own personality; she discovered that she could have a preference for something over something else but, since we did not consider her preferences as defining her, she did not have to hold to them as if they represented who she was. One day she loved carrots and the next she hated them, one day she was a democrat and the next a republican. Since she did not derive value or meaning from either one, she was not stuck with either. If she didn't love carrots, she didn't eat carrots; we didn't lecture her on why she should like them, or remind her that just the day before she had loved them. Resisting anything makes it important. We didn't resist anything so she wasn't stuck with anything. She did not get more attention for liking spinach than she did for disliking it, thus she could do either. She did not need to be consistent, so who she was did not become dependent on her preference for any vegetable.

We did not try to preconceive how she should be, so she could continue to exhibit her flexibility. We, instead, learned from her by trying to become more flexible ourselves. This may sound like it is too easy and too simple, but raising children outside the game is both easy and simple. The kids do the raising. As long as the parent continues to love, include, and not get in the way, the child will prosper.

I am asked the question, "What about the socialization?" About ninety percent of the time, when I tell people we are homeschooling, this is the question I am asked, as if it is their duty as members in good standing. The same way they look at the older child and ask, "How do you like your younger brother?" or they look at a six-year-old and say, "You must be going to school soon."

People don't have to think before they say what they are "supposed" to say. There are so many scripts within a game that hardly anyone ever has to think to say the "right" thing.

The first time I heard the socialization line was when my daughter was less than one. It was from our next door neighbor in the city, a woman who had just told me about the conditions at the inner city elementary school in which she taught. She spoke of stabbings, firearms, drugs, and sex in the hallways. As she explained all this, she did so in a matter-of-fact tone of voice, but when I told her that we would homeschool our daughter, she raised her voice in astonishment, "What about the socialization?" I laughed. She had not been hearing her own previous rendition regarding the state of our schools. Socialization means learning to play the game the way it is being played in the society in which you live. My daughter would not be socialized. She would not be forced to play the game, nor would she be raised by wolves in the north woods, and become a reject who could not get along with anyone. Our neighbor went to school and taught, and then went home to watch TV. Her own teenage son was a juvenile delinquent with whom it was difficult to carry on a conversation; her husband was an unhealthy hermit who, I think, only emerged from the house every third full moon to howl a bit. What has this socialization process really done for her? Yet, hearing that my daughter would grow up without the trauma, agony, and suffering that she had was unthinkable to her.

Now, years later, I marvel at my daughter's ability with people. It doesn't matter if the person is famous or a bum in the street. She treats them with deep respect and curiosity; she loves all people and does each one the highest honor, she learns from them. When she was younger, she was loved and accepted, always. She did not have to shrink, to define herself as something specific. To define yourself is to perpetrate inaccuracy to gain a little bit of what looks like security. To define yourself is to confine yourself, to make specific rules you will adhere to no matter what. Since you are already busy following all kinds of rules within games, the way you define yourself, make yourself an individual, is by having superficial preferences. The more superficial the preferences the better, because they will not contradict a rule. One person likes Ford automobiles, while the other wants a Japanese car. "You have to buy American." Not noticing that the Toyota is built in the United States, it remains a Japanese car. Superficiality is what keeps the nuts dealing only with the protective shell.

Defining who you are is rewarding in that you did it, a personal act in an impersonal world. It also gives you a point of security, a decoy that will appear to be you but really has nothing to do with who you are. People hold to petty preferences; they continue to buy Fords, and are brave enough to let anybody who will listen know all the reasons that Fords are the best car around. Having to obey the rules and stay in the game has forced people to become petty. To create differences that, from the outside, don't even look like differences, and then spend their time arguing about them, is nuts. What is the best restaurant in town? What are your favorite foods? What is your political persuasion? Most people don't even argue about religion or politics, both of which are games with closely defined rules that can really stir up who a person perceives themselves to be. They would rather argue about which sports team is better or how good or bad some musical group is. My scarecrow is better than your scarecrow, my protective shell is better than yours. If you quit being petty just for a little while, you might just discover a lot about who you are. The rules of the petty game is to constantly talk about things that have nothing to do with you as if they are you. The thing about decoys is that the more lifelike they look, the more ducks they will attract. Get excited about some new movie you just saw, or that appliance you have been wanting for years and have finally saved up enough money to get. Consider that you have really arrived when you move into the new house, one of the biggest in town. Have anything appear to be you that has nothing to do with you, and you have protected and defended yourself successfully again.

The process of quitting the petty game is looking at what you really need. One of the things that makes this difficult is that if you have had a waffle iron for a year or two then you really do need the waffles, otherwise you couldn't tell your neighbor that "yes" you had waffles again today. You might have to give up the apron that you had specially tailored that says, "The Waffle Maker" on it. You just might discover that you need very little, and that the more you have the more you lower your quality of life. Remember what a young child needs: food, shelter and love. Not dinner at the French restaurant, just food for the continuance of the body. Not the best house in town, just protection from the elements. Not some symbol of love, but the presence and unconditional acceptance of another person. If a young child doesn't need it and you do, then it is something that you have made up. I am not suggesting that you get rid of anything. I am saying that whatever you define yourself as leads you away from who you are and submerges you, attaches you to an illusion in which you don't exist at all. The result of living within this illusion is a hollow, empty, superficial life.

Not surprisingly, many people ignore the three things that a young child needs. While they may have shelter, many people don't get nutritional food or unconditional love. People have traded what they really need for what they perceive they need. Who you really are cannot need a Ford or Lincoln. But who are you really? A father of three children visited us recently. He was obeying the, "It is good to be busy" rule. Among the work, community involvement, and sporting events he was involved in currently, the family game got lost. He justified this by saying that things would be different in the future, and then purchased snowmobiles for the family so they could have an excuse to spend quality time together.

It is difficult to avoid sarcasm in the face of the stupidity and the naiveté it takes to think that soon things will be different in a specific way; soon you will no longer be too busy for your family so the purchase of some objects will bring the family together. This poor guy trapped in the game thinks he can want something other than what he has. He is alone and busy, caught up in a game. He is unable to speak about anything but the most superficial things with his family. And in a meager attempt to prove that he cares, he goes to a snowmobile dealer.

My daughter has been spared such gestures. I know that if I want to buy something for her, it is usually because I have not been spending enough time with her. I want to replace what I am not giving her with what I can purchase for her. If I make certain that she gets what she really needs: shelter, healthy food, and unconditional love, she will not need anything else. But, if she doesn't get all three of these, then all sorts of distinctions will result, purchases or justifications will follow.

15
Parenting

Games are designed to maximize control and minimize freedom. Parenting by the rules requires that you control your children. You teach them the difference between right and wrong and make certain, at least up to some specific age, that they do the right thing. If your children do not eat a particular vegetable that you think is good for them, you teach them to eat it either by bribing them or threatening them. "You will not get any dessert unless you eat your spinach," or "You can have dessert if you finish your spinach." Both of these amount to the same thing, strong arm tactics and a tying together of spinach and dessert, with you as the dictator who determines the future behaviors of your children. This sort of interaction does not endear your child to spinach, to dessert or to you.

Threats and bribes are well within the confines of the parenting game based on control.

Control is always illusionary. What would happen if you were not in control? Would your child eat only sweets? Would your child die of malnutrition? The best way to ensure that your child will eat well is to eat well yourself. The second best way is to allow your child to eat anything that does not result in death, as much as he or she wants. Control puts you between the person you are attempting to control and the natural consequences of their behaviors. It makes you supposedly superior, and robs the child of learning. Never intervene in anything that will not result in significant injury to your child. That is a rule well outside of the usual parenting rules. Remember that if you quit the game as it is usually played, you get to make up how it is played.

You are sitting at the table and your daughter says she doesn't like potatoes. The appropriate response within the parent game goes something like this, "Potatoes are good for you, you should like potatoes." Then a lecture ensues which, among other things, assumes that when your daughter says that she doesn't like potatoes that is in fact what she means. Somewhere where everyone can read it, it is written that it is good to mean what you say. If you don't mean what you say, you are insincere and, to some degree, criminal and misleading. A child never means what he or she says; he or she is just not so superficial to think that there need be a coordination between speaking and doing. "I do not like potatoes" is an experimental expression to discover what happens when the words are spoken. It doesn't mean anything unless the parent responds in a particular way. If "I don't like potatoes" violates some rule of the parents, then the parent will become the enforcer and teach the child that those particular words did, in fact, mean something. A child is constantly testing, perpetually observing their own responses and the responses of others, trying to discover what increases and what decreases the amount of attention they receive. If "I don't like potatoes" increases the attention they get, it will be repeated at a cost to potato growers everywhere. In discussion with a neighbor or grandparent, the frustrated but also proud parent will say, "Susie doesn't like potatoes." This both defines the child and illustrates a problem for the parents. More accurately, the parent would have to say, "Susie says that she doesn't like potatoes." This only defines what Susie said, and doesn't hold her to a specific position. The appropriate response to the statement about potatoes is a neutral acknowledgment of the statement, to let your daughter know that you have heard it and will in no way alter the amount or kind of attention that you give her based on anything that she says.

This may seem to be a lot of talk about an unimportant point; it isn't. It is the little things that make up the big things. If you try to change or control the big things, you will be frustrated and unhappy most of the time. It is the moments, the tiny building blocks that determine the quality of all life. Potatoes don't really matter, but how you respond in each moment with a child or an adult does matter. Susie could be the sixty-five-year-old woman not liking potatoes, having lived a life by the rule "I don't like potatoes." If forced to eat them once the initial adversarial eat-your-potatoes game is set up, she could even develop an allergy to potatoes.

If you stay within a game, you will have to abide by the rules of that game. The parenting game as it is presently played requires control. If you attempt to control your child, then parenting will be difficult and your child will be alienated from you.

A standard rule of the employment game is that the boss controls you. Games are created to define the lines of control. People thrive in a situation where people are more important than the rules, where loving is more important than games, and where there is never a shortage of anything, particularly attention.

Once upon a time, there was a little boy who loved to sit for hours at the end of his dock and fish. Like any boy, he sat there with his line in the water, thinking about landing the biggest fish in the lake while catching mostly small to medium-sized pan fish. During a time when his family was entertaining a house full of relatives, the boy went out to fish but discovered that his relatives had congregated on the dock, blocking his way to the end. Looking around, the boy noticed that there were gaps between the boards of the dock and began to fish through one of the cracks. He soon realized his mistake when he caught one of the biggest bluegills he had ever seen. It was too big to pull through the crack in the dock. During his attempt to get the big fish onto the dock with the line through the crack the boy lost the bluegill. The next time he dropped his line through the gap in the dock he sat there thinking about catching only small fish. He smiled at the idea of wishing for small fish, an idea that had never occurred to him before.

I learned fishing early in life, from my grandfather. We spent hours together in silence, fishing. I was not allowed to speak or to move, because I might disturb the fish. He taught me about the process of fishing "correctly," which involved infinite patience and the enjoyment of sitting in silence. Fishing, for him, was a meditation to which fish represented an interruption. It was years later, on equipment more advanced than the wooden casting rods and line I had to hang out to dry, that I learned about catching fish. Fishing has nothing to do with fish and everything to do with possibility. You can have a great fishing trip and never catch anything. Though my grandfather and I caught fish from time to time, we learned far more from the process of fishing than we ever could have if we had had to call a stringer full of fish the mark of a successful trip. We often had more communication in our silences than we ever had in words. It was a shared silence, with an occasional interruption to pull in a fish.

Busyness means that attention is focused one place rather than another. It includes the presupposition that there is not enough attention to go around. Everything is vying for your attention. Attention is based on the narrow focus of your awareness and, since it is narrow, you use rules to determine what you should or should not focus on. If you are good for attending to work, then work will receive much of your attention. If you focus your attention on what "is" rather than what "isn't", then you are in the moment and escape from the game. But if you focus on what "isn't" instead of what "is", you lose what is, and your attention as well.

You can only have a limited attention span if there is a limited amount of attention. Time and attention become confused as you become so busy that some things must be included, while most things must be excluded. Attention is awareness focused in a particular direction or upon something. Focus gets you into trouble every time, because when you are focusing on one thing you are not focusing on everything else. In a model based on control, this makes life very difficult. If you are missing more than you are seeing, then control would seem to be impossible. You can only think that you can control what you attend to, thus what you can attend to becomes all there is, and your focus shrinks. You are not able to see the game you are in, because you are too busy attending to whatever part of that game you have decided is most important. You miss the big picture because you are too involved with so many little pictures. If you are busy trying to force your daughter to eat potatoes or like potatoes, you might miss that you don't like squash. If you are even crazier, you will also try to get your daughter to eat squash even though you don't like it.

If your daughter has to eat potatoes, then you have to have squash every time she has potatoes. That's fair. You have grown up wounded, which means with preferences that you have been locked into, limitations that you perceive to be who you are. The opportunity of parenting, if you quit the standard game, is to have your daughter teach you about your limitations rather than forcing your limitations on her. Parenting can be about you expanding to fit your child's lack of worldly distinctions, rather than your child shrinking to fit yours. This expansion is sufficiently threatening that most parents avoid it. If you get a book about parenting, it will almost surely be a book written by someone who is attempting to legitimatize the control of children.

Quit attempting to control anything and you will discover that you blossom. Control is so pervasive in our culture, and in the nature of games themselves, that it is difficult to see it. If a sound persists long enough, you no longer hear that sound; that is the way it is with control. Parenting is the perfect place to escape from control, because it includes one player who has not yet adopted the party line and one that has. Thus, the one that has can perceive him or herself through the eyes of a child. To the child, the parent is a god. What kind of a god do you want to be? Do you want to be an all-knowing all-powerful tyrant who enforces his or her will (the control model), or do you want to be a loving accepting god who notices the little things but is willing to love unconditionally? The power to define your child's deities is a power that each parent has. How big do you want your gods to be? The bigger your gods are, the bigger you can be. Nobody ever gets bigger than their gods, it just isn't allowed. Since you are your child's god how about becoming infinite yourself? God obeys no rules, would God want less for you? Would God give you rules, or would man acting as a god give you rules? The idea of an infinite being bothering to create a species and then defining how that species must behave is too ridiculous, yet it is taught everyday. You define your child's deities each day in the way you behave, in what you include and what you exclude, in what you accept and what you decline, in each moment of your life. How big a god will you be?

16

Chain of Command

Q

Lou has it tough. He was sexually abused and treated poorly as a child, which according to him, led to alcoholism. He is allergic to grass and lint, and currently lives next to a golf course. Around the age of twelve, Lou started doing drugs and getting acne, both of which have scarred him for life. He was elected homecoming queen in his senior year of high school, a humiliation he never sought or wanted, and he was singled out as the least likely to succeed, not because he wasn't bright, but because nobody liked him. He spent four years collecting baseball cards. His collection contained practically every card ever printed until one evening, while he was asleep, his mother accidentally washed his collection in her old ringer washer. With the loss of his baseball cards, Lou began to collect addictions. It took him nineteen months to learn about and acquire every addiction known to humankind except two. He had finally found his niche.

Right out of high school, he got a job at a fast food hamburger restaurant, but was fired after three weeks for cursing at the french fries in front of customers. Having been fired from more jobs than there are in a town of two thousand people, Lou's longest position ever held was as a tester at a clothespin factory. Hanging clothes all day, and then submitting them to different wind speeds to test how well the pins held, was Lou's career for two entire months, until he was fired for drug use and insubordination. He has worked through a lot, and is now drug and alcohol free. He is in his late fifties and, for the first time in fifty years, Lou likes himself. He has gone through so much and has come out alive, happy, healthy, and spiritual in spite of (or because of) his traumas.

Lou's twin brother Ivan has led a very different life. Ivan was left on the doorstep of a rich and happy couple's home hours after his birth, taken in, and promptly adopted into high society. Though he was not born with a silver spoon in his mouth, he had one as soon as he was old enough to eat solid food. Ivan was loved and cared for by his adoptive parents who had been wanting a child and had been unable to conceive. Ivan was just what his parents wanted and needed and, in turn, gave Ivan every material thing anyone could want. But his myriad of possessions paled in comparison to the love and affection his parents showed him daily. Ivan went to the best schools and was a straight "A" student. At Harvard, Ivan received his doctorate with a double major in business and Latin, while lettering in tennis and football. Upon graduation from Harvard, Ivan married his high school sweetheart, Rachel, and took over the family businesses, building them far beyond anything his father could imagine. By the time he was forty, Ivan owned the mansion next to his parents, where he and Rachel lived with their two well-adjusted healthy children. He worked on the average of ten and a half days a month, spending the rest of the time with his family playing and traveling.

Ivan's days were filled with exploration and reflection, delighting in anything and nothing in particular, while contributing to the people around him and the world as a whole. He was given an honorary cover picture in the world issue of *Who's Who*.

They were sixty-two when Lou's road of struggle, passion, and hardship crossed Ivan's path of love, passion, and discovery. Ivan was at the United Nations, receiving the Humanitarian of the Century award, when Lou, having written down the wrong address for Sara's Wishy-Washy, where he was applying for a position as a bleach person, accidentally bumped into Ivan in front of the UN building. Lou was in a brown JC Penny work uniform (brand new), and Ivan was wearing a tuxedo. In spite of their different backgrounds, foregrounds, and interests, they liked each other instantly, and became fast friends and companions for the rest of their lives (thirty-some years.) They enjoyed a friendship and attraction that neither of them

ever understood, while never discovering they were brothers.

Different games have different rules, often conflicting
rules. You wouldn't play the same golf hole over and over,
but what about monogamy? "The two are different," you
might say. Imagine if the rules of golf required playing the
same hole. You would soon get bored and disinterested,
you would play less golf and probably divorce the game.
Boredom is often the result of repetitive rules. Variation
keeps us playing, and rules almost always restrict variation. The overall objective of all games is to limit you as
much as they can, but not so much that you quit playing.
The only threat to the games is your quitting. What if you
were only allowed to play golf with one club?

Calling games different allows different rules to apply at one time or location than at another. This complicated process demands organization and interferes with
generalization while restricting learning. Generalization
allows cross-context movement of knowledge and is eco-
nomical both in terms of time and energy. But it threatens
the separation between games. Games stress differences
instead of connections, so it is no wonder that loneliness
and alienation result. Generalization is "bad" people say
when they are seeking to shrink and specialize. Generalization is "good" when they apply learning from one field
appropriately to another.

Physicists don't often hang around with artists or chem-
ists, and probably stay a goodly distance away from min-
isters, at least in their line of work. The basic presupposi-

tion that has us miss connections and isolate ourselves is that things are different. Everything is whole, there is no difference. Remember the mandatory rule of wholeness? That one thing is different from another is absurd, but believed by almost everyone. Games depend on and accentuate difference; it is the very food that sustains them.

What is the chain of command that determines value for us? We have to know what value is, or there is no game. Value is the process of making something more important than something else. Value is a very tender breakable thing, both brittle and fragile. It constantly must be fed or it starves to death, and everything becomes the same, worth the same amount of attention, money, time, or whatever else you are gambling with in your game. What is the final link in the chain of command that defines how important or worthwhile the chain is? Even the words *important* and *worthwhile* get in the way, because they are potentially part of the chain. By chain, I mean the sequence of importance, each step of which leads closer to a declaration that something is valuable, worth playing for. You might not walk across a shaky bridge for a nickel, but you might for twenty dollars or a million dollars. What it takes to get you to cross the bridge depends on your *perception* of several things—the condition of the bridge, the consequences of failure, every other such event you ever engaged in, and how much you need the money. A simple game like crossing a bridge becomes very complicated. No game is as simple as it seems, and no game is as simple as you think it is. So much individualized perception mixes with expertise in every game, that it takes a tremendous amount of courage to play, unless you have no alternative but to play.

A typical chain starts with wholeness and moves quickly to difference, of two things that are perceived differently. One must be better than the other. The criteria that you use for good varies. It might include what is more useful, what makes you look better to others, or what is similar to other things that you have said you liked. There are so many links that lead you to finally declaring something valuable. The process takes place so quickly that it is almost impossible to tease out. A subtle chain is DNA, while a more obvious one is emotions, while yet another more blatant one is your life story. Each seeks to differentiate "you" from others at different levels of subtlety. The final link in a chain is where value is created; all the links that lead up to that justify the final addition of value. The preceding links obscure your authorship of the value, and appear to make value intrinsic. The final value determines people's relationship to the whole chain, and they become an effect of the chain.

The complication of this structure reveals one of the oldest rules there is, "Thou shalt not question the chain of command," which is another way of saying, don't question the structure of games, rules, and presuppositions. Never, under any circumstances, question the game. Just get busy and keep playing. The game, any game, will not survive persistent questioning. The worth of the game will ultimately, or sooner, reveal itself as created—as illusion.

Even writing this stuff wounds me, offends what little structure I have left, because as a soldier, which you are if you defend anything, you must never question the chain of command. Follow your orders and the order will be maintained.

Are you the leader, or just another person defending a fox hole, idea, position, or cause? All games consist of defining a chain of command, and all rules seek to reinforce and ensure the persistence of that chain. To question any chain of command is to strike against order itself.

Difference requires time, which leads to sequence; then control, order, and existence are born. This is an example of a chain, and try as I might, I can't make any sense of it. As a foot soldier, you are supposed to just follow order (orders), not question or attempt to understand it.

Q

With a little nervousness, Dad and I headed for the high pasture, a place I had dreamed about for years and was finally going to see. I took a long breath of crisp morning air, while I remembered all of the conversations with Dad before he finally gave his permission for the trip. We were really setting out for the high pasture, and I was going to see the free and wild horses who have never known the cut of a bridle or the weight of a saddle. These were unbroken horses. The very mounts we were riding had come from the high pasture. Long ago, they had been wild horses, but now they were good horses, meaning they knew their job and they did it. They carried us to and from town, got us to the Saturday night dance and back, and on this day, these same horses were taking us to their old home and hopefully back to our home again.

We rode hard for the first part of the day, and finally arrived at the high meadow. It was a long way from the house, but still part of the ranch. Though I had never been there before, I recognized it right off from all of Dad's stories. Dad both loved and feared the open expanse. It was endless, and nothing like the lush fields nearer home. As I looked closer, I saw grasses, shrubs, and wildflowers I had never seen before. The very vastness of the high plain struck me physically. It was hard to imagine that there could be a place so much larger than all of the places I had ever seen put together. I gasped for breath at the spectacle in front of me, and heard Dad do the same thing. I seemed very small and unimportant, as I gazed up into the enormous sky that stretched out in all directions guarding the ocean of endless waving grasses. There were no horses in sight, but we were in no hurry, since we had set aside several days for our visit to the great high plain.

We made a small yet adequate camp, bringing a little bit of home to a strange and scary place. The familiar bed rolls and dinner rolls made our temporary camp seem almost significant. We fixed a quick lunch, speaking little while we hurriedly ate, with great anticipation of the adventure ahead.

It was time. We headed out in search of the wild horses. Though we covered a lot of ground during the first day of our search, our only discovery was some day-old droppings. The horses must have known we were coming. Either they had a kind of sixth sense about these things, or the high pasture was so big that it would take some time to find them. Dad preferred the *so big* explanation, while I thought it a good deal more likely that the horses knew we were coming long before we arrived.

Mid-afternoon of our second day, we saw our first wild horses. There were ten of them, with a magnificent looking chestnut brown stallion in the lead. We watched the dignified animals for a long time, proud of ourselves for finding them, and realizing only too well the work that was still ahead. The chase began. Dad rode toward the group from the east, while I headed in from the west, hoping to separate at least a few of the horses from the leader. Our chances of overpowering a single horse while they moved together in a pack were nigh on impossible. It seemed odd to be chasing after wild horses, knowing that the horse I rode was once as wild and free as the spirited beasts running in front of us. Our plan worked. On the first try we managed to separate three of the horses from the fold—two beautiful mares and one fine young stallion. It took us about an hour to corner and rope the mares, with the stallion being young enough to follow his mother.

At that point we had a decision to make. Should we try to get more horses, or head for home early with the three we had? We had been luckier than usual to get three horses on the first try, and three beautiful specimens they were. We decided (Dad decided) that we had enough for one visit, and that it was time to head for home. "It will take long enough just to break these three, son," he said. "At some point we'll be glad we settled for three." He was right, but I only found that out later. At the time, I wanted more horses. I wanted the lead stallion. I had pictures of myself riding into town on the back of that sleek brown steed, the proud owner of the best looking horse around. I didn't think about the difficulties involved in breaking him, which should have been my indication that he was not to be mine. I had never heard of anyone capturing a wild lead stallion alive, though I knew of rustlers who would shoot the lead stallion to make it easier to catch the followers.

We headed for home, exhausted and proud. The newly-captured horses were jumpy as we left the high pasture, a place that had always been their home. I turned for one last look at the vast plain, vowing to return again next year, and perhaps to make it my home someday. Until then, the pictures I had stored of the great sky and the endless prairie would have to do. The trip home was exhilarating and entertaining, as we kept our high-spirited captives in check. When the wild horses trotted along willingly, we rode in silence broken only by the voiceless conversations I was already rehearsing in my head about talking Dad into another trip next year. We arrived home with the three wild horses, and a permanent impression of the high pasture in our minds.

The horses were difficult to break, and did not take easily to domestic life. They shied away from us and resisted any attempt we made to touch them, but time was on our side. After several relentless months of rewarding them with soothing talk and sweet things to eat, and punishing them with the sharp snap of a whip, they were willing to at least act like domestic horses. I viewed the process with mixed emotions. It was a challenge to break them, but at the same time, I wanted them to resist being broken. Once domesticated, a wild horse was no more interesting to me than the horses we already had. I entertained the idea of keeping one of the horses wild, an idea Dad would not go along with. He said, "You break wild horses, that's what you do. When they are wild they are no good to anyone, no one but themselves leastwise." I knew it would be no use to argue, but Dad was wrong. I knew it because any time I was a little scared or worried, I would remember that wild stallion, and my fears and concerns would leave as quickly as they had come. Thinking of that wild chestnut brown beauty was of much more use to me than all of the domesticated horses put together. I used that brown stallion the rest of my life to urge me on when things got tough. While never owning up to the pictures I made of myself riding into town on the back of that sleek brown stallion, I still owed him a debt of gratitude for the wildness he reminded me of in myself.

My first book was finally in our hands, accompanied by the expectation that many people might really like to read it. Luckily, we had room for the three thousand books that the printer delivered to us. Now what? Never had I purchased so many books with the same title by the same author. What my personal library lacked in variation, it more than made up for in quantity. We mailed to people, talked to people on the phone and in person. Over the first year we sold about fifteen hundred books. The process was slow. The books attracted people to us who had contributions to make, people who wanted to learn, and people who could teach us. It would be two years before I would write my second book. In that time, I learned how to write effortlessly outside of time. I didn't learn this through practice or consulting experts. I learned it by getting curious about how much fun writing could be.

People learn through inactivity, between events, not during them. There is learning everywhere. I thought I knew how people would respond to the book; I didn't. The moment you think you know anything, you had best prepare yourself for a fall. The very act of knowing is claiming a certain ability within a game.

17

You Must Think You Are Free

Imagine attempting to play one game while wearing equipment from another game.

In his shoulder pads and helmet he felt safe; there would be little chance of injury today. He got hit only twice throughout the game, and those two hits were because he could not get out of the way fast enough. He was defeated in straight sets, but at least he was safe. His game seemed to be a little off, his timing was behind, and the pads seemed to get in the way of swinging his racquet, while the helmet blocked his vision somewhat.

It is difficult to bring rules from one game and apply them to another; it is even more problematic to attempt to make up new rules to an old game. If you keep playing the games you have always played, you will probably end up very similar to how you are now. Your situation may change, but you will remain much the same. Ignorance of the rules is never an excuse within a game. If you are going to play, you had better know the rules. One of the big problems is that there are so many rules that it is impossible to keep track of all of them.

A few years ago the game of football underwent some rule changes, such as the reviewing of plays by instant replay. In baseball, there was the switch to a designated hitter. Many years ago, the voting law was expanded to include women and black people. When the rules change, people sound a lot like camels being loaded with one more item, one more thing to carry. People use the rules to lean on; they count on the rules. A rule about rules is, don't change the rules.

A person can play only so many games at one time; to do otherwise is to play each game poorly or to go crazy. The game called parenting has certain rules, while the game called career has other rules. Very creative individuals manage to juggle both of these games at the same time, obeying both sets of rules, but most people don't. Balancing different games at the same time always means compromise in one game or the other and usually both. Rules change in order to accommodate the coordination of games. Seventy-five years ago, career and parenting only worked when one spouse had a career and the other spouse did most of the parenting. Today, parenting seems to have little to do with being around children. Daycare or school takes over the days, while TV, friends, or a baby-sitter takes care of the evenings. The shift in the rules has allowed both spouses to work and still call themselves parents, whether they remember the names of their children or not. Whether the shift in rules is good or bad, it is like everything else, a matter of perspective.

Before John F. Kennedy, there was an unspoken rule that Roman Catholics could not become President. Before Bill Clinton, blatant and admitted adultery, or using illegal drugs, would tend to keep a person out of office. Rules change, games change, and presuppositions occasionally change.

Games narrow what one is able to perceive. Creating a new game requires the broadest possible perspective. Thus, continuing existing games often precludes making up new ones. Denying that one is playing a game does not exempt one from following the rules of that game, but it allows the presuppositions and most of the rules of that game to become habitual and thus invisible to the compliant player. Extracting oneself from a game has so many repercussions, that it takes rigor and time to do so. Only a broken rule, or one that you are about ready to break, becomes obvious.

Rules relate to how something is to be done, while presuppositions have to do with what or who is doing. Thus, presuppositions are about existence, while rules relate to doing. Doing relates to action, while existence relates to being. What something is often seems to be easier to determine than what is done. But, how one goes about determining what something is reaches to the deepest assumptions that provide the foundations for a life. Questioning what you did is much more polite than deeply pondering who you are. Opinions are rampant regarding what is "good" and "bad" behavior, what one should do and what one should not. And there are rules that prohibit the goodness or badness of the very thing itself.

Are you a saint or a sinner? Even more importantly, what determines which you are? Who or what dictates your life? If you could stop thinking that you are free, then you might see that you are enslaved. If you are really free and think that you are not, there is no problem. But, if you think that you are free when you are not, then life becomes one problem after another. Do you have any problems?

The heroin addict doesn't like heroin; he or she likes the results that heroin produces in them. More than likely, the heroin addict hates heroin because it dominates life, dictates all behavior, and eliminates the illusion of choice. This is exactly how it is with rules. People hate rules, but they like the illusionary security that rules seem to provide. They are willing to give up certain rights, as long as their neighbor also gives up those rights. They might want to shoot their neighbor, but there is a rule against that, which thankfully also stops the neighbor from shooting them unless, of course, the neighbor is a policeman.

People hate the rules, and they love the rules. They are ambivalent to the presuppositions because they don't ever see them. To have an opinion about something, you have to perceive that it exists, and most people don't perceive their presuppositions. People love to be told what to do, because then they don't have to worry about what to do; and they hate to be told what to do, because then they are no longer free to do what they want. The history of rules goes back to the first human being. So, obviously, rules are important. This love-hate relationship with rules ensures their continued existence. People have created a way to live with rules, which is to act in accordance with them while pretending that rules don't exist. Ignoring rules does not make them go away; it just gives them complete control. Looking deeply at a rule, observing all its effects and all it attempts to control, threatens the existence of that rule. To assist in not looking at the rules, you have distracted yourselves. You attend to *stories* instead of rules. You explain the things that you do with stories that have nothing to do with the rules. You do this because of some reason, and do that because of some other reason. The suggestion that you should look at the rules that dictate your life is not a pleasant one. As fast as rules are obeyed, stories to obscure the rules are created. You want to know why the criminal killed someone, rather than just notice that he or she did. You want everyone else to obey the rules, but if they don't, you want to know why they didn't, which distracts you from looking at the initial rule. Stories protect rules from being exposed as rules.

Any explanation that you give for anything is an attempt to stop you from seeing that you acted in accordance with some rule. The rule determined what you did, but that is difficult to admit. If rules dictate what you do, then you are not free. There is a rule in the American game that says, "You must think you are free." Rules don't need evidence, but people need evidence. If you have a bloodhound, and you give the dog the shirt off your back, he won't run very far to find you. Rules are so close to home, that you have to constantly reach beyond them to discover explanations for their lack of existence. "If you want to get somewhere, you may as well start where you are," seems too practical a rule to follow. The stories that you tell detract you from where you are and lead you away from yourself. If you systematically take apart your stories, rather then building or repeating them, you will discover that you have left a trail that leads you back to the rules that are guiding your life. If you then follow the list of rules back by perceiving each one and its repercussions, you will arrive at the presuppositions. If you look deeply into each presupposition, you will discover that it was created by you and has no reality of its own. At the moment that you see nothing, the presupposition will fall away, and you will discover that there is no you, and that everything is you. At that moment, you will be complete, whole, and totally blissful. You will be the universe in love with itself. You will be clean, empty, full, and free. You will glow without effort. The process of discovering who you are is not easy because, paranoid as it sounds, nobody wants you to do it.

If you didn't have to prove, or even make, your initial presuppositions, the games would not result; there would be no rules, and there would be no stories to hide the rules. You would be left to play gameless, a free agent able to create your own deal with any team or no team at all. What kind of object has no sides? The moment that you take sides, or even perceive sides, there is an object other than you. This sticks you with an objective and a perspective that puts you in a certain relation, which restricts all you say, do, and think. This process occurs so fast that it takes all sorts of little quittings to see it. The thing about a chain is that it can be broken anywhere and its continuation ceases. You are chained. Quitting breaks those chains. You are chained in so many places that you don't dare see the chains. There are so many more rules about what you don't see, than there are about what you can see, that you are lonely, but it doesn't have to be this way.

Following these trails back to their sources can be fun, scary, exciting, impossible, or anything else. It all depends on you, as does everything. The moment that you realize it all depends on you, you will be set free from thinking that it all depends on you, and you can begin quitting.

The process of quitting leads to learning. Learning is discovering what you don't know and then losing it. Any attention to what you do know just slows you down and gets in the way of this process.

Q

After a while you come to a fast-moving, treacherous looking stream. There are rocks in the stream, but it is difficult to determine which, if any, will hold your weight. You want to be brave, but this is scary. A child might view your plight as a playful adventure and spend a great day with the stream. As an adult, you are faced with a serious situation—you must get to the other side and remain dry.

You test a rock, it seems sturdy enough, and unluckily it holds your weight. Unluckily, because the more rocks that hold your weight, the more likely you consider the next one will too. This is why statistics were invented, to assist you in losing while winning. If there are a certain number of secure rocks, and a specific number of insecure ones, each secure rock you find makes it more likely the next will be insecure. Thus, you win by losing and you learn to distrust.

A moose comes by and stumbles through the stream. He didn't have a rule about staying dry and passed you by. If you have a gun, you shoot the moose; that ought to slow him down and pay him back for not obeying your rule.

After several attempts to cross the stream and remain dry, you get wet feet and quite tired—not physically, but mentally tired. It is difficult to remember which rocks are firm, safe, and which are not; you have begun to doubt yourself. Learning isn't easy, especially when there are consequences for not learning. You need a way to mark the good rocks and the bad ones. This will relieve you of the burden of learning, or remembering. You could put a little mud on each good rock, and thus tell at a glance which rocks you can count on. Charcoal or chalk would be better, in that they would last longer and be less apt to wash off or get there by accident. A chisel would be even better from the standpoint of longevity, but would be difficult to work with. However, its permanence (the Rosetta Stone) just may make the effort worthwhile. A printing press would be even better. You could map the rocks, make a representation on paper of which rocks are safe and which ones are not. By making a map, you go beyond your initial crossing to contribute to the ease of future crossings, while also setting up the possibility of a lucrative map business. But, the even bigger jump is that your map creates symbolism, something representing something else. In the future, you and other people who had your map would be free from having to remember the nuances of each rock. The chiseled marks reduced what you had to remember to one thing, the mark that indicated safety, but the map has you look at the stream in relation to the representation. The representation becomes more important than the rocks and the stream. So, the accuracy of the map, and your ability to interpret abstract symbols rather than the stream itself, determines your safety. The map costs you your relationship with the rocks and the stream, but only so long as the stream stays the same. Variation in the stream is the enemy of the map. All of a sudden, in a selfless attempt to have yourself and everyone else who needs to cross the river do so safely, you have become an opponent to change. The stream can change, but your map will not. The stream will change, which leads you to define danger as the rate of change. The more the river changes, the more often it will have to be remapped. Change is danger, and thus you become afraid of change.

The printing press has allowed you to divorce your safety from the rocks themselves and place it on the accuracy of the map. You have become a symbolic creature who is no longer responsible. Now the map and its maker are responsible for your safe crossing. The map will always be more consistent than the terrain. It could even be confused with the terrain.

Knowing which rocks are secure and which are not reduces the risk, but it also reduces the adventure and learning. There is still the original discovery phase that is necessary, though, and that remains risky. Precision becomes necessary, and any person crossing the stream by map is only as safe as both the consistency of the stream and the accuracy of the person who made the map.

The more people who cross, the less risk will be tolerated. Let's build a bridge. Force order on the rocks. Fasten them together in a certain structure, then you don't need to pay any attention at all and you will never get wet. Soon you don't even notice the stream. You drive over it, you race past it, thinking of your destination or of something that happened last night or last year. You can now cross the stream in a trance, in a daze. Practicality has taken over, and the stream and a sense of adventure have disappeared for you. Meanwhile, a child is still playing in the stream, adventuring and learning. The weekend warrior is still crossing the stream without the bridge or a map. And the bridge is ever so slowly falling apart. The rocks are randomly returning to the stream, a return to risk and adventure.

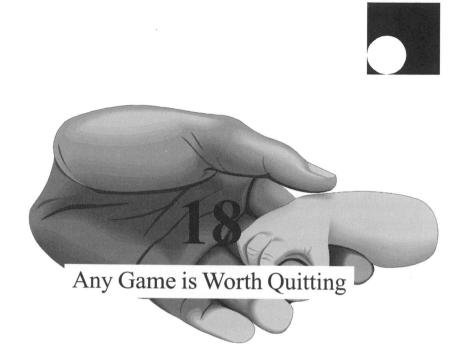

Any Game is Worth Quitting

As the games continued to fall away, lightness replaced them along with the ability to create my own games, ones I wanted to play instead of ones that I had to play. Through examining my life, and being willing to quit anything, I discovered more of what I didn't know I had lost. Any game is worth quitting. If you perceive a game as a game and can quit it, then you don't have to. Ecology is the science of how games fit together, both within a person and between people.

My daughter was in her late four's when my wife and I decided it was time to have another child. It was not culture who decided it for us. Nobody told us to have another child. It was our game to have one. With our first child, we had followed the rules of pregnancy. These required visits to the doctor treating pregnancy as a kind of sickness, the duration of which was nine months. We even attended a birthing class, once, to learn the rules of the childbirth game. Pervading the class was the rule that pregnancy is uncomfortable, leading up to tremendous discomfort at birth. We never went back to that class. So, in my daughter's birth, we broke some of the rules; my wife didn't need to have discomfort or pain and so she didn't. We obeyed the rule that birth needs to happen in a hospital. The doctor, panicked during the birth, grabbed my daughter's arm and pulled her out. In the process of doing so he separated some nerves in her right arm. For four months, she had no movement in the arm; and for the next three months, she could only move it toward her body, never lift it. It seems that in a difficult situation there is a greater tendency to lean on the rules, a kind of search for security. We went to a specialist who dealt with such conditions; he really knew the rules. He wanted our daughter to wear a plastic contraption which was velcroed around her middle. At the very least, the device would ensure that the first year of my daughter's life was uncomfortable. Quickly we ignored him, massaged and attended to my daughter's arm almost constantly, and now, years later, it is almost impossible to tell which arm was pulled.

An expert is a person who has learned a lot about a specific game, and is familiar with most of the rules. A master is someone who knows all the rules and presuppositions and recognizes them for what they are, which makes the whole game optional.

Our next child would not be born in a hospital. We found a midwife who did not play by the rules, or at least had rules that we were willing to play by. Her rules included that childbirth is a natural easy event, a part of life no different from any other. She promised us that she would attend the birth, and would not do anything other than bring the expertise of having attended hundreds of births. She would come and be an advocate of everything working easily and perfectly during the process.

The night of the birth came. Labor was a bit deceptive in that it lasted only a couple of hours. I called the midwife, who lives about an hour away, and told her that I thought it was time. My daughter woke up about five minutes before we saw the lights of the midwife's car coming up the driveway. The midwife walked in, looked at my wife, and said, "Push, here it comes." Within five minutes of her arrival, the baby's head showed. Quickly, the baby came half way out and stopped. It gasped for breath once, then again. The midwife said that the baby would not try to breathe again. She stood and watched. The baby was dying, not breathing, and yet she did nothing. She obeyed her rule that childbirth is natural and that it just works. She kept her promise to us not to do anything. At moments like this, which is all moments of your life given that life and death are so close together, there must be one person present who maintains the rules of a game that works. That is what our midwife did.

Within about a minute our son came out; the moment that he emerged completely, the midwife began CPR and gave him oxygen. For over a minute he did not breathe as we cheered him on to do so. He was blue, and the room was full of cheering. Finally, he breathed, and then began breathing in earnest. I don't know what would have happened if we had been obeying the hospital birth rules, but I don't know any way that the birth could have been better. If you are going to play a game, then make certain that the rules of that game are ones you can live with. Rules that further life contribute not to who you perceive yourself to be, but to the whole range of what you can perceive, and to the variation of that perception to the largest degree possible.

Two children are even more fun and educational than one. If one child can tear your life apart, a second can make unrecognizable all the pieces that are left over. We questioned the rules of child-rearing with our daughter, but with our son there were no rules. Examining led to disappearance as it always will. We were no longer amateur parents; we were empty vessels, willing to play and dance all of the time. Imagine growing up with two unconditionally loving parents who consider you to be perfect exactly the way you are, and who constantly move out of the way of your endless drive to learn. Our rules of parenting had not changed as much as they had become practically invisible. "The child is always completely included and accepted" became our only rule.

The fewer the rules, the easier they are to follow. The hierarchy of illusion is built with rules intended to enforce other rules. Our rules replaced enforcement with the appreciation and acceptance of oneself, so there was nothing in the way of giving to the child. This may sound easy, but remember that almost all rules arise out of fear and laziness. When you are the least bit weak or doubtful, the rules give you something to fall back on, that you can count on. We had nothing to fall back on, just the momentary existence of love. A question that I kept hearing in my head was, "Is it possible to love someone too much?"

Occasionally, rules from other games would invite themselves into our game: you shouldn't spend too much time with your child, let your child cry it out, you and your wife need to get away from the children sometimes, don't do that, if you do that again you will be punished. There are endless dictates that fall out of a game. Even though one has quit a game, there are still invitations back into that game. Some of these invitations are tempting, but most of them look ridiculous.

With two children, the process of quitting sped up, and it was even easier to live outside of culturally defined games. My daughter helped significantly by playing with her brother. She continually showed us that the child-rearing game worked that we had played while raising her. This encouraged us to refine and demolish it. My daughter learns so fast, and loves other people so much, that we were continually encouraged to extend beyond the game we used with her, and even have fewer rules and less structure in my son's way. The kids constantly urge us onward, not so much by what they say, but by how they behave. It is by their blossoming outside rules that they reveal the rules we have left. Rules are a bit like fertilizer; they are a waste product that can be used to encourage new growth as they decompose. Rules are useful, and never more useful than once they are discarded. Elimination is an essential part of human existence, and quitting is mental elimination.

19

The Mandatory Game—The Present

Perhaps I have picked on optional games enough, perhaps not. Every time you play an optional game, you argue for the reality of that game. The purpose of all optional games is accounting: to figure out where you stand, and to make yourself "important" and "right." Obviously the most relevant an optional game can make you, if you remember it is a game, is optional. To be more important, you have to forget that it is optional, and, further, forget it is a game at all. There is no value or importance in a game.

There are some games that work much better than others. Most of these will not even look like games to you. One of these is living in the present. Chances are you have already quit this game; you do any*time* you focus on the past or the future. The present game is a game you are always playing, whether or not you perceive that you are.

A presupposition of the present game is that everything is whole and complete. A rule of the game is, "There is only now." In other words all is present, if not accounted for. Remember, a game is making what isn't more important than what is, so technically this is not a game, but it underlies all games. The present underlies everything.

The penalty for quitting the present game is the loss of perception of the present, and entry into a world of past and/or future full of games based on illusion. This is an extreme punishment that you have learned to live with, sort of. You have redefined living as playing different games and made the best of your punishment, your exile from the moment. All games are an attempt to distract you from, to justify, your loss. They are fundamental attempts to create reality. Reality doesn't need to be created, it already is. Within optional games there is no reality. Reality is simple. The games get more and more complicated the more you play. If you play long enough or hard enough, optional games appear to be mandatory, and that is the basis of justification.

Games devolve; they move from simple to complex. A child is quite content with moving a block from one location to another; initially a child is content without moving anything. An adult requires much greater distraction than does the child. Entertainment doesn't come easily within complex games. As I quit other games and began making up my own, I noticed that my games had fewer and fewer rules; they either remained simple, or I quit them. The simpler the game, the less attention you have to expend trying to follow the rules. Chess is a very different game from checkers. In checkers, all of the pieces must move in one direction, until they become kings, and you always have to jump. In chess, each piece has its unique moves, and all taking is optional. You lose in chess when you cannot move anywhere without being taken, in other words, when you are the most restricted. The more complicated a game, the more it attracts you, and the better you perceive yourself to be for playing it. There are very few people who define themselves as professional checker players, while there are many serious chess players. People must fill their time and distract themselves. Chess, by its complication, is a better distraction than checkers.

The moment that you exit the moment, you perceive the illusion time. You must fill the time that you perceive you have. Too much time is a threat, so you must get an occupation and be occupied. When you are in the moment, there is no time, thus, occupation and games become unnecessary. Games are an attempt to fill time. Some games are called work, and some are called play, but their objective is the same: to kill time.

There is nothing worse than having nothing to do. Often leisure becomes even busier than work time. A structure of intricate and infinitely tempting games awaits you on the other side of the door that leads you out of the present. In the present, you only exist; there is no perception of you, because that would require you to be something other than you perceive yourself to be. In the present, all that you have called you disappears, so does good and bad. You can't know where you stand in the present, because you stand everywhere and are everything. The present is totally inclusive, and it is always where you are. When you break the rule, even in your perceptions of the present, you've bought the big lie, "There is something other than the present." Illusion is based on this lie. It is this faulty foundation that makes illusion, all of the optional games, so precarious. It is because you play them all the time, and because they are so precarious, that you must consider them important. In the present, nothing is more important than anything else. There is no importance.

The temptation is too great. There is the door; all that is beyond beckons you, it screams to you, it offers you anything you really want if you just leave the present for a moment. Just open the door and look out, take a peek. If you open the door, you see time stretching behind and out ahead. You are swept into a world of complication, and you must seek to regain your balance, to discover where you stand. Everything on the other side of the door, outside of the present, is created, made up, manufactured and fabricated by you to keep yourself busy figuring out where you are, what you are, and who you are. But, who you are within the illusion has no relation to who you really are. Each moment is a temptation to leave the present. You are an addict, with that which you are addicted to always available but never present; it is no wonder you are as frustrated as can be.

Once you exit the present you have no now, so you have lost all that is for what can be or what you can create. You have plenty of time to do your creating, too much time. But you quickly discover that this is not a world of only your design. It is a garbage dump full of games that millions of other people have designed. You can't turn around without bumping into other peoples' presuppositions, rules, and games. You are not free to create, because there are not many raw materials around. After thousands of years of illusion building, there is so little raw material left.

If you need to know where you stand, then you can be certain that you are in an illusion, and it is only in illusion, in optional games, that you can be certain or uncertain. I don't know how to communicate in words what living in the present is like, because it isn't like anything; it has no peers. You have probably had moments when you were in a perfect world, when you experienced that everything was in order, as it should be—bliss beyond, far beyond, comparison. That and more is the present, without any identifying of anything.

The root of insecurity is illusion. The games let you know where you stand within the illusion, where you stand in relation to other players. If you make up a game from scratch, you will not know how you compare with others, because nobody is competing with you. In the present, there is no competition, because competition requires separation.

In the present, life is easy and there are no problems at all. Life is perfect. In the world of games, there are constant tests that you must pass; vigilance is required to play, and quitting appears to be death. When you have identified yourself as illusion, ending illusion looks like the death of you. If it doesn't mean anything, then what is the point? There is no point, there is no meaning, there is no importance, not really. Life is too easy in the present, so let the games begin.

There are so many essences of games because there are so many games. A game is where all differences are accentuated to their maximum, and, when there is the greatest threat of them disappearing altogether, you back off slightly. If a football player never got hurt, you might well question whether he was giving the game all he had. You have to go beyond your limits, hit harder than you think you can; that is where really good game players play, and that is where pain and injury occurs. Thus, to be a really good game player, you must get hurt. It is little wonder that there is so much pain around. Within games, pain is as close to real as you can get, and it indicates that you really played hard. "No pain, no gain." The worse it hurts, the better you play, and the more you push yourselves.

In the present, there is no pain, and there is nothing to gain.

The fewer rules your games have, the more they look like the present game with one presupposition and one rule. When you quit sufficiently to be able to create your own games, you might want to make sure to model them after the present game. Keep them simple; the fewer presuppositions and rules you create, the less apt you are to be lost in illusion.

When you make something important, which is what you are doing even if you stumble onto something that you think really is important, it won't be long before you consider that thing to be who you are. After you quit enough games, you get to start making up games. If you play a game that somebody else defined, you will probably become a lot like the other person. Within the games, the games define you. The loop of all games is complete when the last link, importance, goes full circle and becomes who you are. Since you must be important, and there is something that you have found that you think is really important, then you must be that thing. After all, you share importance. Revealed, this sounds illogical, but in action it is diabolical and invisible. Everybody who makes anything important plays this game; it is the way that the most superficial elements of life come to define you, who you are. It is the way that the least important rule you follow influences your deepest and best hidden presuppositions.

The universal objective of all games is to have you be important, make you appear good, to be good, or have you win. In a world based on difference, like the world of illusion (optional games), this is not easily accomplished. At a young age, you discover that, no matter how fast you run, there is always someone who will run faster. No matter how smart you are, there is always somebody smarter. Your defense against the loss of not being the best is to define yourself so narrowly that within your tiny game, within the rules you make important, you are the best. To do this, you overlap and interlock games and define importance and winning in constantly narrowing ways. You become smaller because it helps you win. Certainly Jack can bake a cake better than I can, but he can't write like I do. Mary is president of the company, but I know things that she doesn't, and she doesn't spend nearly enough time with her kids, not as much time as I do. Games are all about shrinking, especially if you have to win. Competition, you are taught, helps you to do your best. It does just the opposite. It locks you into relative goodness.

The temptation to prove yourself is so great that you enter the games. In the world of games, you must win a few and lose a few, but you must, in some way, always perceive yourself as a winner. Thus, you distort the distortion all in the name of winning. In the present, there is no win and there is no loss; the game is over.

Lose the moment and you ignore mandatory games for optional games. You don't really lose the moment; you can't, except in the world of illusion. Play the games, but return to the present. Quit enough games, and you are free to create games. But, return to the present. The present is the peak experience, but it leads to your peeking out the door again. The closer you come to the present, the more ridiculous games look. The trail of rules and presuppositions will lead you through the tangle of games all the way back to the present. You will then be playing only the game that you are always playing anyway, only ironically you won't know it. In the present, you don't know anything; you only know everything. You don't recognize only one connection; you become all connections. The good news is that you are there already, you have already arrived; the bad news is that you don't know it.

20
The Special Combination

To win any game, or all games, with so many people playing, you must come up with a unique combination of presuppositions and rules. All the sensible, logical combinations are already taken, so you put together a bizarre and complicated one where the overlap of games is just right. "I only like broccoli if it is cooked in a white pan with Yak butter." Aren't you unique and unusual, an individual like no other? An interesting person. This special combination defines you, and seems to give you life. It verifies the illusion, and makes you appear important in the face of all the evidence to the contrary. Who cares that it is so superficial that it can't matter to anyone? It matters to you, and it will matter to anyone who is worthy of being in relationship with you.

Imagine an old pocket watch, one of those gold ones with all the jewels inside. The precision of it is impressive. Now imagine taking it apart. What tools would you need to take it apart? Vice grips, while being one of my favorite tools for most jobs, would not be very useful, neither would a large ball peen hammer or even a regular sized screwdriver. You would need special small and delicate tools that resemble the precision of the watch you want to use them on. You might want a series of tiny screwdrivers, each one smaller than the one before it. You might need little tweezers.

If the idea was just to take the watch apart, you could probably do that quickly, but the game here is to take it apart, put it back together again, and still have it work. You had better pay attention while you are taking it apart, and you had better treat each newly removed piece with respect. Without any one of the pieces, the watch will not work the way it once did. "Take your time" would be a good rule here. Rushing ahead will probably cause you problems later, and is not recommended. Too much time might have you forget where the pieces go, though, so it might be best to work at a reasonable and steady pace.

This is not a race; it is a combination of precision with memory. It is the interest in finding out what makes the watch tick, without damaging the watch so it will never tick again. If you accomplish this task, you will never again look at your watch in quite the same way. You will have an intimacy and understanding of your watch. You will know what makes it tick, and you will be the maker who is responsible for every tick, once you have put it back together.

To dismantle the watch, you must both care if it works again and have a sense of abandon even to tackle the job. Many people would not take the watch apart as long as it is working. Even if it were not working too well, they would put up with a certain amount of inconsistency to avoid taking the watch apart. If it stops entirely, they would take it to a watch repair man, being too afraid to tackle the job themselves. A child would be interested in taking the watch apart strictly from curiosity, while many adults would shy away from the task in the name of practicality. After all, the passing of time is not something you are qualified to fool around with.

Your special combination limits you. It means that you can't really enjoy broccoli any other way. It means that your own particular spin keeps you busy attending to it, but busy is good. The special combination that defines you is also the combination that keeps others from unlocking you to discover who you really are. It protects you from them but it also isolates you from them. It isolates you from yourself, and protects you or hinders you from finding out who you are. Superficial relationship is a game of continually trying to unlock the other person—to discover their unique combination.

It is lonely to be unique; it is also entirely artificial, a construct of yours that isn't real and doesn't exist. Illusion is oppressive; reality never is. Optional games must prove they are important. Mandatory games are beyond all that. In optional games you must win, which is difficult. This pulls you along by the nose to a strange and lonely existence as a slave, no longer free, to the games you must play.

The way to stop playing is to quit. An alteration of how you are playing will only lend some variation within the illusion, some change. This will always create more difference, and will never return you to the whole. As a whole person, there is no difference, and illusion is irrelevant. You are not unique; you are completely connected and related, you are free, and you don't care who knows it. You have nothing to prove. The same people who are willing to try to discover your combination of presuppositions and rules will probably not be interested in your wholeness.

If someone likes you because of your preference for broccoli a certain way, then you must not change your preference or they may not like you. This might sound ridiculous, but many marriages fall apart, or friendships disappear, over such superficial issues. If people like you for some reason, excuse, or combination of presuppositions and rules, then they don't like you, they like the reason. Quitting means removing yourself from the rules, discovering and then losing the presuppositions, not playing the game anymore. If people liked you for the game, then quitting will have you disappear for them. If they liked your illusion, and you lose your illusion, then they will not even recognize you. If someone liked you because you played racquetball with them, and you quit racquetball, then you probably won't spend much time together, or you will have to discover some other reason for your friendship. If people like you because you are worried about them or want to help them, then you must remain worried or wanting to help, otherwise the foundation disappears. Nobody wants you to quit when they consider you to be your combination of rules and presuppositions. If what I am saying here sounds too superficial to be real, it is probably because it is. It is not real.

Do your parents like you because they are your parents and you are their child? If so, then the rules of the game that they call parenting must stay in place no matter how old you get. If the rules are lost, the relationship, as you and they know it, is lost. Parents who are holding onto the relationship by holding onto the game are threatened by your growth or any change in your life. The very idea that you might find out who you really are is so deeply threatening that it is unthinkable, unperceivable. Would your parents want to be around you if you were not their child? If they met you on the street, would they invite you over for the holidays? Would you want to spend time with them if they were not your parents? One of the rules of the parents game is, "Thou shalt love thy parents." Another rule is that, no matter what you do, you are still the child and they are still the parents. Most parenting games define the parents as controllers and the child as the one controlled; it is little wonder that so many people break the rule about loving their parents. Many people hate their parents. If you hate your parents, the rule is, "Thou shalt not show it." There are rules for everything. If you hate your parents for some particular reason, it is not your parents you hate but the reason. The same with love.

Love is a function of inclusion, it has nothing to do with reason. Love is often entirely unreasonable. Discovering someone's unique combination is giving them attention for what they have managed to exclude. Uniqueness and/or winning are games of exclusion. They have nothing to do with love. You might build walls around the city because you don't want to hurt the person on the other side of your walls, but more likely you do so to protect yourself. Reasons cloud the rules. Whatever the reason, any reason has you not able to perceive the rule that is on the other side of the reason. This set-up contributes to perceiving illusion as real. Behind every reason is a rule you don't want to look at, that threatens the illusion or a presupposition you are afraid is true. Within the illusion, reason is in the way of perception; it justifies without clarifying. It pollutes without remorse, so that you will only see part of your illusion and miss the rest. The more you quit, the less reasonable and the more intelligent you become. The less you focus on just a few connections, the more connections you are able to perceive. The world opens up for you as you quit.

If someone is agonizing over something petty, you can be certain there is something much bigger underneath it causing the problem. People are not oysters; the protective shells they build around their problems or perceived soft spots do not turn them into pearls. They close you off from other people and from yourself. They define you and limit you; defining is always limiting. The oyster does not prize the pearl; the pearl is, at best, an inconvenience to the oyster.

Within the world of games, there is only unreal satisfaction, and there is no love. That doesn't mean that you can't call something love or think that it is love. It means that you have misidentified something as love that is not.

Within optional games, people kill other people who do not play by the rules. Monogamy is an optional game, and how many people have died in an attempt to prove that it is mandatory? The less important a rule is, the bigger the penalty must be attached to it to make it look important. To have it look real, the penalty must be incredibly harsh and exercised quickly and universally. The rules and presuppositions of mandatory games are everywhere always. To mimic this universality, try to apply *some* rules *everywhere*. In the American game, attempts at universal rules are called the Constitution and its amendments. In religion, they are the good book, specifically the ten commandments. All optional rules and presuppositions are still open to interpretation, no matter how long they have been around and no matter how serious the consequences for breaking or ignoring them.

One of the most universal rules about games is, "They must go on." A game, in order to be a really important game, must not end. If it ends, there is a gap that must be filled. As long as a game goes on, it is open to interpretation and thus, over time, reason will have its way with every game. Every game will ultimately, if not sooner, become unworkable through the efforts of each individual to win that game. The complexity of illusion will continue to increase, and the game will become more and more limiting. The game leaves reality farther behind. Reality is simple; games are complex.

The rule about rules is, "You must have rules." The rule about presuppositions is, "This is true." The more often a rule is followed, the more real that rule appears to people. The more often a presupposition is considered true, the more legitimate it becomes. If you have a rule that you abide by but nobody else does, you will not fit in. You will be considered odd. But if you can convince other people to abide by your rule, you then have company, or a company. Your game mixes with their games with more or less ease, and the game of games continues.

There is nothing wrong with games, and there is nothing right with games either. The problem with games is that people forget that they are games. When you confuse limitation with reality, you confuse who you think you are with who you are. You shrink beyond recognition. You get caught up in the details and superficialities of life, and miss the game by thinking that it is not a game. Games can be fun and, to some degree, even rewarding, if you can continue to recognize them as games. A society in which people take recreation seriously will not have an easy time distinguishing optional from mandatory games. The moment you confuse a game with who you are, or make anything more important than mandatory games, you lose everything that is, and must quickly lean on everything that isn't. What isn't is not supportive at all, it is the root of all of your insecurities. In mandatory games, nobody wins or loses. An addiction to an optional game makes that game all important. This addiction makes you crazy for more, and seems to make you unable to quit. Quitting looks like death, and thankfully death comes along sooner or later to relieve you of your burden. Within the world of games, death is a threat, the end of the game, the end of your opportunity to define importance. It is just that, but, within the mandatory game, death, along with everything else, is nothing.

Basically, all games are intent upon proving what is— what is you, what is important, what reality is. What is already is and it needs no proof, thus the games are unnecessary. What is is, it doesn't need you to figure out who you are or even be who you are. The game is over. The only way that it doesn't look as if it is over is for the fans to stay in the stadium and the players to stay on the field, for people to keep running around breaking up things so that somebody has to put them back together again. Humpty.

21

The Craziness of Illusion—Revealed

You are funny. But you often miss the joke. You escape from the moment to find a world of illusion, to live out your wildest fantasies, and then limit yourself as much as possible. But, within an illusion, it is not necessary to limit yourself at all. Technically, it makes sense within an illusion to explore all possibilities; that just might be the purpose of illusion. You can explore things in illusion that you wouldn't dare in real life. But if you define illusion as real life and real life as illusion, you will have things quite backward and not discover yourself at all.

Any*time* other than the present allows you to avoid responsibility and accountability. It leads you into the world of illusion where nothing matters and you can do no harm. It is a bit like a padded cell for a crazy person. It doesn't matter how many imaginary things the crazy person has in the cell with him or herself, no damage can be done, only perceived damage. To perceive something as damaged or good or bad takes a tremendously narrow focus, a loss of the whole. When you have lost the whole, you have lost everything, and games take on significance.

Games determine how you can interact with people. Games determine what you do almost every waking moment of every day. You are the games; thus, there is no you left. Life without games is life without rules; it is freedom. Planet Earth has a few rules, but nothing compared with the rules that people have forced on themselves. Life without rules is light, and no stories are necessary. There is nothing to justify, and nothing to prove. Only play exists outside of games. Anything is possible outside of games, while only limited possibilities exist within games.

The more games that I quit, the fewer rules demanded a response, and the easier life became. Until you quit a few things, it is impossible to conceive of how oppressive games are. There are games that govern everything, and each game has so many rules that soon life becomes entirely defined. You know what you must do and what you must not do, with such little variation you don't even need to be awake to wander through life. Each rule makes you a little less relevant, a little less important, and a little less alive. Without rules, the world is an incredible place to play, an endless dance.

Football is football because of the rules. Consider football without its rules and it is no longer football. Football isn't life; football is football. This may seem like a simple point, but it is worth noticing because it is so often missed. Anything that you think is life, or think is a part of life, is not life. Life is independent of games, and has nothing to do with stories, rules, or presuppositions. The very idea of voluntary limitations is repugnant to nature and evolution. How much fun are you allowed to have? This is a question that resides within a game. How much fun you *can* have is discovered outside of games.

Life is wonderful, easy, and undefined. The traumas that people experience can happen only within games. Win and lose can happen only within games. Suffering can happen only within games. Without games, you stand everywhere, so you need have no concern about where you stand. Within games, the main purpose of games is to determine where you stand. It is the nature of a game that, when you discover where you stand, then you also learn that there is somewhere else that you should stand. It is the discontent that results from this internally determined disappointment that builds up to suffering and trauma. The suffering also results from the game determining where you stand, rather than you determining it. Games keep people busy, but they also keep them from discovering who they are. A game is always smaller than life and smaller than any person playing it, thus a game is always restrictive. The limitations of games rob you of life; so the more games you are involved in, the less life you have.

Look at the games you play, and you may just get your sense of humor back. You leave the present, and then invent money to get you back to the present; you can't buy your way back to the present, but you think you can. Otherwise, why would money be referred to as currency? Current is the present, so money must be an attempt to make you accountable like you were in the present. If you don't have enough money, you can get credit, which has you lose accountability again and no longer need to remain current.

You have to keep up with what is going on in the world, even though what is going on in the world keeps changing. Keeping up with what is going on means that you must trust somebody that you don't even know, such as the reporter, newscaster, or camera man. You are supposed to ignore what is going on in your immediate surroundings, which could have you discover a lot about yourself, and attend to what somebody else says in the moment.

I took part in a march when Martin Luther King was killed. At that march, there were thousands of people, and one person with a sign which had some slogan written on it opposing the march. The next day, the local newspaper had a picture of the person carrying the sign. If you had not been at the event, you might have thought that the picture was in some way representative. Do you want to trust someone you don't know whose job is dependent on your continuing to watch? Craziness is demanded of people every day, but it doesn't seem crazy because people are stuck with the game, not knowing it is a game.

You stay home when you are sick, and go to work when you are well. You take care of yourself when you are sick, giving sickness attention, and pretty much ignore yourself when you are well. Sickness brings on a tenderness from which you can learn about yourself, and cuts through the blinding normalcy of every day. But instead of taking advantage of this opportunity to explore your tenderness, you go to a doctor's office, with other sick people, where someone you trust more than yourself tells you what is going on. You turn over to someone else your ability to perceive yourself, and pay them a lot of money for the distraction they provide. A hundred years ago, a doctor was a person you needed if you were about to die, and the doctor didn't get paid well. Today, the doctor stays in his or her office, is consulted about every trivial imbalance, and is paid huge sums of money. The doctor doesn't trust him or herself, so equipment is necessary to determine your condition. Even if the doctor wants to trust, he or she can't, because you reserve the right to trust him or her and then turn around later and prove that your trust was poorly placed, and all that happened to you is really the doctor's fault. Malpractice is the back door to trusting the doctor, and justifies the fees. A dollar gets nicked as many times as people can figure out how to do so.

The three little kittens, they lost their mittens. But, luckily it was covered by their homeowners policy. Insurance is an attempt to shelter you from the consequences of your actions. It used to be that if you lost something, it was gone and you needed to fend for yourself or ask a neighbor for help. Insurance has made help mandatory. If your neighbor has the same insurer you do, then when you make a claim and your neighbor does not, you are taking money from your neighbor. Part of his premium or much more than his premium comes to you. But, insurance is not looked at this way, so the neighbor is robbed of the perception that they helped you, and you are encouraged to make as many claims as possible. If nothing bad happens to you, then you have been supporting other people's problems for all the years that you have paid premiums.

It doesn't matter which of our games you look at, you can strip down the rules to discover the real nature of the game. What is lost and what is won in the game is seldom revealed with just a superficial glance at the game. What is rewarded in most games is some continuation of the game.

All the games are crazy. Every game is crazy, thus everybody playing also must be crazy. You have to get out of the games to look at the games. While you are obeying or resisting the rules of a game, you are supporting that game.

From outside, you can choose to play a game or not, and you can create another game. But from inside the game, all games limit your perception sufficiently that you will keep playing. Quit, and discover who you are not. Quit, and chances are very good that there are other people supporting the existence of the game so you can always return to it. If, some time after quitting, you still wish to return to the game then do so, but know that it is a game. If you can't walk away, then you are addicted. You have, to some degree, wrapped up your existence with the game. The heroin addict is the heroin. The two are inseparable. Addiction defines the inability to separate who one is from that which one is addicted to. If you can't quit your job, then you are addicted; you have become your job. How much of your awareness and attention does your job take? What are you giving up (selling) to work? If you are your job, then you are selling yourself. Prostitution is the oldest occupation, and it will keep you busy.

There is nothing wrong with working, unless you have to. There is nothing wrong with playing any game, unless you have to. There is nothing wrong with holding any opinion or point of view, unless you have to. The 'have to' in all of these cases means that you have so connected what you are doing with who you are that they are inseparable. If what you perceive yourself to be is less than everything, then you are wounded, injured, and abused. You have confused what isn't with what is, as you attempted to make what wasn't more important than what was. You have moved games to the level of presuppositions and, in doing so, lost who you are, confusing who you are with the game. You have, in short, lost by playing, by having to play. You have already exited the present, and you would have to exit the illusion, optional games, to get the perception of present again. Until you do, you will continue to suffer and derive your worth from emptiness, defining sustenance as starvation, and value as deprivation. You will play the downside, thinking that it is the upside. And being human, you will make the best of it. You will soldier on under a burden that you do not need to carry, that you are not carrying at all. You will think that you are carrying the weight of the world while carrying nothing at all. You are free to go, and you have all of the reasons necessary to keep you there. The warden, you, has opened your cell door and invited you to leave, to recognize the freedom you have always had and never enjoyed, but you are too busy to leave. There is work to be done. Everything that you have to do is work. You are addicted to your cell, because you have finally gotten it almost exactly the way you want it, well not quite the way you want it, but you are working on it.

You have made a difference in your cell, and you will make no difference outside of it. This prison is over-crowded because nobody wants to leave. The conditions in the prison are awful, but everybody is so used to them that they stay. At least they can complain about the conditions and maybe, just maybe, contribute to conditions being slightly better for the next prisoner. You invite your kids to visit you in prison. No children are born in prison; they need to be coerced into going there, and then they have to be convinced that they really should remain. Once they have been there long enough, they, like you, have no life outside of prison. They remain there, not with you but busy along with you. The prisoner who stays in prison because the door is locked at least can blame someone else for being there. But it takes a much thinner excuse, a lot of thinking and faith, for the prisoner who could be free to justify captivity. Basically, you are taught that you do not deserve to be free, and that you already are free, a contradiction that costs you the perspective of what freedom is, thus you stay in prison. Nobody deserves to be free, but nobody deserves to be in prison either.

The strange thing about this prison is that it only exists if you say it does, believe it does, and think it does. To leave, you must see what you are doing, see where you perceive yourself to be, and then quit. The very act of looking reveals so much. Follow the trail of rules out of the prison, continue to walk the line of presuppositions, and you will discover the present. You will be present. The prison will have disappeared, but it will also continue to call to you, to invite you back. If you go back, which you probably will, you can go back on your terms, and you need never stay so long that you forget who you are and who you are not.

22

Dismantling the Structures of Games: Presuppositions, Rules and Stories

Stories

Rules

Presuppositions

A basic rule included in almost all games is, "You must be in control or at least think that you are." Yet, the greatest thrills in any game come when you are right at the edge of losing control. To bowl perfectly, you have to think a lot while training; but then you must get your mind out of the way, so you can bowl the same perfect ball over and over. Mountain climbing is best when you are right at the edge. It is you, because of your ability, who is able to hold on in the face of extreme adversity. Just when you are ready to lose control, if you can still hold it, then you get a sense of exhilaration. The exhilaration is not from gaining control, it is from being so close to losing it. If you did not gain back the control or the illusion of control, then you would enter the present. It is in the face of adversity that control must be retained.

What you think you want is not what you want. Who you think you are is not who you are. What you think is just what you think. Thinking becomes all important outside of the moment. In the present, thinking plays no role. Thinking is an attempt to control. Control exerts itself anywhere, without even taking on a form. It starts with the creation of difference. Anything that you can divide, you can control. Divide and conquer. There is no control in the whole, thus the whole must be split up.

You are here to tame the wild, to break the horse so that it is in your service. You cannot really control anything, of course you can't, a fact that does not stop you from trying. You move through life, leaving rules where you perceive you have already proved your control, and enter unknown terrain. You try to live within some kind of equilibrium in an ever-changing world; now that is crazy. Anything you cannot control upsets you. Upset means that you are not in control, or there is some threat to your illusion of control. Ironically, when you are upset, you might discover who you really are. Upset is your best friend but seems to be your worst enemy.

You cannot control, but must. So, you opt for perception; you see yourself in control. That is the way into the world of games, the heavily traveled path. If you didn't need to be in control, you could see that you were not. If you could see that you were not in control, you could be entertained, you could relax and play. If you trusted that everything would turn out the way it does, and not have to have it turn out some other way, you would be constantly entertained. If you didn't need to see the control that isn't you, you could stop projecting yourself everywhere and discover where you are.

Parenting seemed to be a game that I must not quit. Most people's children are problematic enough that they are not even tempted to like them too much. All the quitting I have done has resulted in having children who are so incredible that I never want to leave them. They are heavenly, and from heaven there is nowhere to get to. Thus, when I am in their presence, I want to remain there forever. If I hold to them, though, they don't stay wonderful; I *have* to be around them, and then being around them becomes work. I can see them as gods or I can see them as devils; it all depends on what I have to prove. If I am in the moment, I have nothing to prove. Their attention spans are endless because they are in the present. The past and future require energy to attend to, thus children who try to attend to them get tired and become distracted.

It is the very games that you must keep playing that wear you out so that you cannot keep playing them. You chase your tail, and chase your tales, as you attempt to figure out everything one thing at a time. Figure out, identify, define, construct, accomplish, and manage are all euphemisms for control. Controlling that which does not exist is hard work; before you can control it, you must think that it exists. If you are scientific, you must prove that it exists. If you are religious, you just have faith that it exists. But mostly, by being human, you just assume that the people who came before you and proved or trusted that it existed were right. Enough has been thought that you really don't have to think anymore. There is no need and little reward for having an original thought. Creativity is not rewarded within structure. Sufficient structures have already been created, so all you have to do is learn to play by the rules. It is radical to do otherwise.

The structure that exists will support the status quo. You are always voting either for illusion or reality. Your votes for illusion must be counted, but your votes for reality don't matter. If you vote for illusion, optional games, then you can be important; if you vote for reality, you cannot. It is little wonder that the world of games is so tempting. People who don't even enjoy playing keep playing, because there is something to prove. Being as imperfect as you perceive yourself to be would necessitate your always being busy, and continually trying to prove that you are not imperfect. This smacks of control. You can't be in control of some things but not of others; you are either in control or not. But, being in control of everything means total responsibility; you would be back to the whole again. So you think that you are in control of some things, but not others, and you seek to extend your perceived influence.

You don't have to choose to play the mandatory game, being present, but life is easier if you do. You do have to choose to play an optional game, and life is more difficult if you don't (if, instead, you view the optional as mandatory).

Control takes so many different forms. Buying something is control. Try not buying anything for a year; you will discover that every little purchase is an argument for your control. Try interacting with other people without control; have no preference for how they are or how they perceive you.

Watch yourself make a decision. Decide means to kill off alternatives. Watch yourself kill off alternatives. Catch those reasons as they work, and you will discover the rules. Decide to go out to eat. Forget how you made that decision, but now focus on where you should eat. You have to go to a restaurant that is within a certain distance, different distances for different people. Some people would consider thirty miles to be close, while others would never go that far; yet others might drive several hours to get to their favorite restaurant. The farther away your favorite restaurant is, the more time you can kill driving there. So get a map and draw a circle that includes the distance you are willing to go to dinner. Notice if you think that the farther you drive, the better the meal had better be to make the drive worthwhile. Nobody drives hundreds of miles to go to a lousy restaurant; that is why there are so many McDonalds.

The circle is drawn. Notice that you might be willing to go outside the circle if you had a really good reason for doing so, such as a new restaurant that opened thirty-one miles away and your circle is at thirty miles, but you have a new girlfriend/boyfriend who might be impressed by going to that particular restaurant. In addition, they have a two-for-one which would save you some money, but you don't want to look cheap. The thing about rules is that they are all negotiable; and, as long as you are negotiating them, you are oppressed by them. So you decide to break the thirty-mile rule and go to the restaurant, because it might impress your girlfriend/boyfriend and save you money. Everything within a game, in this case the "Where is dinner to be eaten?" game, is done for a reason. Pick a restaurant that you have no reason to go to and go there. That is not so easy unless you have never been to that restaurant before, and you have the reason that you have not been to it. Remember that presuppositions come first, then rules, and finally stories (reasons).

Try to pick a restaurant based on no reasons. "Pick" is a euphemism for control. Go to a restaurant different from all other restaurants you have ever gone to, or order meals you have never eaten. It is difficult and odd to strip away the layers that are built up regarding even the simplest decision. The process of doing so is enough to make you crazy. It doesn't really make you crazy; it reveals that you are operating on top of craziness almost all the time, and don't know it until you examine some of what you have built.

The process of dismantling the structures of games: presuppositions, rules and stories, is often difficult; but it will always result in your having more energy and more freedom. It will lead you back to a simpler time when you didn't need so much and you were not nearly so needy. The day's happiness depended on so little. Now, with the complexities that have been created, it depends on so much. Happiness has become fragile, as it requires so many parts. Nothing survives the moment; thus, maintaining anything is impossible. To a child, the simple is more than enough.

A box is a wonderful plaything for a child because it is pure possibility. What is in the box is a limitation until it is removed from the box. When you are in a box, a box constrained by the structure, there is little room to move and few possibilities. While this may appear safe, it is the least safe place there is. The more limited you are, the more fearful you will become, and you will call yourself secure. Illusion attempts unsuccessfully to keep the poles of paradox apart, and between the poles let the games begin. But, let them also end. Quit, and you will discover that paradox is the ultimate in entertainment. It also is proof for your connection to everything. Start looking for proof of your connection, instead of evidence for your control, and your world will expand approximating its real size. You can play here, but playing is optional. You can work here, but working is optional. Anything that appears mandatory to you is optional because, really, mandatory will never appear to you at all; it is you.

23

Disassembly

Once you start questioning the stories you are telling to cover up the rules that you are wrestling with, only to discover the assumptions you have made about who you are, you will discover that this process takes on a life of its own. Changing the rules will not help anything; enforcing rules will not make you act well or make you happy. All that presuppositions, rules, and stories can do for you is have you lose sight of who you are. At best, they limit your possibilities, and, at worst, they catch you up in the automaticity that needs rules to determine what forms your existence should take. Don't change the rules; question the ruler. You are the ruler; question yourself. If you are deeply involved in a game not of your own making, you will need to quit that before you get on with exploring yourself. The people who want to change the game from within it will only get more stuck in the game. There is a temptation to become distracted from the game, even in an attempt to get out of it.

Imagine everything in the world, every single thing. Picture strings between all of these things, everything connected to everything else, an intricate weave, a patchwork of connection. Everything that there is is attached to you, and every thought that you have is attached to everything and to every thought of every person. Even the things that seem to have passed on are here and connected to everything. Imagine the string being white, shorter and longer pieces of string, depending on how far apart things are. The strings expand and contract to allow all of the movement that occurs. Now see the strings remaining attached but slowly becoming every color in succession, moving through the spectrum and spanning the rainbow, and finally becoming clear, invisible. You can't see the connections anymore. Everything is separate and alone as far as you can see. This is what happens when you leave the present, the connections disappear. As you look very closely, you can still see the connections, but not if you, in any way, interfere with the connection by trying to make a connection. You can perceive a connection for a moment if you focus exclusively for a fraction of a second, but then that connection disappears again. You can never see it long enough for your mind to be certain that you saw it, but you did see it. You can either trust your mind that you saw it, or not trust it and assume that it is you who must make the connections, or assume that they do not exist. The latter assumption occupies your time, it keeps you busy.

All work is intended to create or maintain a connection. A VCR is a certain connection between things that did not occur naturally; it is a subset of all connections, with attention just paid to a few. The price you pay for the VCR justifies focusing on a specific group of connections and ignoring others. It takes energy to focus on some connections; it takes nothing to focus on all connections. Soon you only see the connections you have made, and you see them whether or not you are looking at them. Your home-made connections can be carried in your head; they never existed outside your head anyway. The very act of placing them and then storing them in your head changes them in all sorts of little ways. These changes are so subtle that you can't distinguish them without a real connection as a reference. You live your life trying to avoid even one real reference, because a real reference would indicate how far off the trail you have gone. Soon you call real what you are carrying in your head. You become the connections in your head. To keep your "reality" safe requires all kind of rules. For insurance, you have children and friends so you can encourage them to take on your "reality."

You take the connections in your head as basic assumptions, and then build a game composed of rules to defend them. You don't know the whole set-up is a game. If you did, you would laugh more often and be well all the time. You become an evangelist for your reality, because it is the right reality. Your game is the right game. To prove your reality, you must limit what you can see and what you can do. You must restrict your perception of who you are.

Somebody appears who is not part of your reality, who isn't playing your game by your rules. Their momentary appearance is a threat, because they are aware of different connections than you are. They have manufactured their reality, and it is nothing like yours. This idea is too disturbing for you to see. You are motivated and driven to defend and perpetuate your game. You are now alone, unable to relate even to yourself because you lost yourself so long ago. You lost yourself too many steps back to start over. And the only way that you can be right now is to continue in the direction you are going.

You must look good, you must be right so your internal world mutates independently of the outside world. You create a world, your world, and live in it. Certainly it is lonely, but it also seems so safe. You are this game, but you don't know it is make believe, imaginary. So, as you must, you do the best you can. You are brave enough to continue on, but not to turn back. Reason directs you forward. All of what you have considered yourself to be would be lost if you turned back now, if you quit.

Occasionally, your perfection shines through. But it makes the illusion look so bad, the only way to appreciate it is to suspend good and bad along with your whole imaginary world. That suspension is quitting. Your internal world will not end, but it will at least be recognized, re-thought, as what it is. This way, by quitting, you can discover who you are. You can then shine, glow, and play only the games that you make up and want to play.

24

February 17, 1990

The more of my time that a game consumed, the more difficult it was to quit. The more of my thought a game consumed, the more difficult it was to quit. The combination of these two conspired to have me consider my very existence dependent on or even be the game. As I examined and quit games, I discovered there were still more games to quit. Thinking back to the structure of my first workshop, and the total free-form of my workshops now, the freedom is obvious. The more I was dependent upon, the less I trusted, and the more certain I was of specific things in lieu of everything. I knew the right answers; now there is no such thing as a right answer.

Some results of quitting were slow coming, while others came in a flash. February 17, 1990 was one of the flash days. I was leading a workshop in Atlanta, Georgia, when I noticed that I was at the edge of tears. All day throughout the workshop I was very tender. Since there didn't need to be a reason for this tenderness or the tears in my eyes, I was able to just observe it. Thoughts of my family raced through my mind. By early evening, the invitation was clear; I was to quit my family. Quit my family? What a crazy thought; what an odd necessity. My wife was everything I wanted in a wife, and more; my three-year-old daughter was the most important human being in my life, the center of my existence. For a moment, I resisted quitting and the tears flowed. I accepted quitting and the laughter started. It was really this easy to tell the difference between what I should quit and what I should not. Laughter and tears were so close together, indicating the simple difference between slavery and freedom. What had seemed to be a line that required much thought to discover, now became obvious. I was to quit my family.

I accepted, and laughed and laughed like a crazy person, a person who let go of something that he could not let go of. This quitting my family did not mean that I had to leave my family or denounce them; ironically, it resulted in my spending much more time with them. What it meant is that I could no longer define myself as a father or a husband. I could no longer play with family as a game of limitation. It is trite to say that, at that point, my family grew from a little nest of three of us to the entire universe, but it is true. My daughter and wife were free from any burden of expectation I had placed on them. They no longer had to behave in any particular way, or think in any set way. Our relationship was no longer dependent on performance or structure, and I was no longer dependent upon them. They did not, could not, define me; neither could I define them. The subtlety in quitting became more obvious to me. Quitting doesn't require movement or even change, it involves that release of an illegitimate attachment, of making something important in lieu of something else. When I released dependence on the family, on specific ties, then I could watch my daughter grow, rather than attempt to control her growth. I had already quit attempting to control her learning. The biggest gift we can give to another is the release of all control over them, letting go of expectation, all expectation. The moment I quit the family, my wife and daughter appeared perfect to me for the first time. Not perfect because of something, but perfect in their existence.

Glimpsing perfection required letting it go. Coincidentally, our host in Atlanta had laid out dinner for us on a long table that looked much like representations that I have seen of the Last Supper. I even said it, "Here is the Last Supper." By the end of dinner, it was the end of all of my resistance to quitting, the termination of all separation, and the beginning of complete openness and trust. The energy coursed through me as I explained to the people at the table, which included my wife and daughter, that I was leaving and never coming back, and that it would look as if I was not going anywhere. The words were spoken by me, but they were not filtered by me. At the time they made sense to me, but I didn't know where they came from. They were not what I should have said or what I should not have said, but out they came. The words revealed my future to me as I told it to them. They would have to take over as I left, and I would become less able to function within the world of games. This was a turning point where quitting took over, and no stories ever needed to be believed again or rules followed blindly. The process of giving up my family had freed me sufficiently that the gravity of my life was now pulling me toward freedom. Quitting no longer took effort; it happened naturally. Life from that evening on became a flow, a flow that could be trusted and embraced, a flow that would continually offer me who I was and knock down who I might perceive myself to be. Quitting had led me to the point of no return; I could not go back, and I did not want to.

Everything in my life changed that evening, yet all that had happened in my life led to that change. The change was extreme to me, and to those who knew me well, but was virtually unobservable by anyone else. The change was in perspective or, rather, the speed at which I could perceive. I gave up control and knowing, and discovered that these two had continually slowed down every thought that went through my head. It was by the desire to control, and the need to know, that I had slowed down the racing thought; and with the slowness had come the temptation to stop the thought altogether, and hold on to it as a part of who I was. I had been giving up control for some time, but to give up knowing was a much more subtle level of release. The more subtle the release, the greater the flow that ensues. The gross is gross by its few connections, while the subtle influences everything. I was free of knowing; knowing evades trust. It is a clever euphemism for control. The moment I gave up knowing, the thoughts raced through my head so fast that I couldn't identify, or identify with, any of them. I discovered that it was by their slowness that they blocked traffic, and resulted in the irritation that I had always called myself. The result of this release was the end to internal conversations; the voice in my head was silent and peace reigned. I could now sit for hours, days, and probably even months doing nothing and totally undisturbed.

Meditation was something that I always wanted to do but never could. It now became necessary for me to meditate. My specific meditation meant lying down with nothing to do and nothing to think. It was not sleep, it was not anything. Always before when I had attempted to meditate, thoughts had raced through my head, mundane, sometimes odd thoughts, but something had always been there. Now thoughts flew by untethered and unnoticed, thus peace reigned. I meditated often, and when I did not do so often enough, my head would begin to hurt. The headache would at times become so painful that I had to meditate, or it seemed that I would die. Physical symptoms will always lead you to what is next for you, if you will let them. Wondering if it was time to meditate was a thought that occurred sometimes, and if I ignored it two or three times, it would be joined by the sensation I interpret as eagle claws tearing my head apart. With a quiet mind, and the release of the need to know, came a natural knowing that made life effortless.

Over the next few days, the permanence of my new lack of existence became obvious. I had visions; in retrospect it seems that they were either rewards or temptations—rewards for quitting and reaching the point of no return, or temptations to hold on to or think that this time I had really crossed the line into craziness. Jesus visited me one night, and with him was a man in white robes whose face I could not see. They were discussing me briefly. I never had religious training, but still knew Jesus instantly. It was not his features that revealed him to me but his presence. He made himself known to me outside of my senses, in a much deeper way, beyond perception. As the vision disappeared, Jesus spoke, "You are doing fine; don't bother me again." Without sufficient preparation, I suppose this vision could have tempted me either to think I was blessed, or to commit myself to an institution. I did neither, because craziness or blessedness both require a backdrop of presuppositions, rules, and stories that I no longer possessed. Thus they no longer possessed me, so even a vision so clear and potentially touching was no more relevant than the bowl of fruit I ate the next morning for breakfast. The visitation was a matter of fact, and meant nothing. I had numerous other at least as striking visions and visits, but let each go as fast as they occurred. The very act of releasing one made room for another. Ecstasy resulted for several months, to be followed by agony.

The agony was, of course, the next quitting. I had made peace with my mind; now it was time to make peace with my body, or at least lose the line between mind and body sufficiently that my mind did not need to separate or control the body. Your biggest fear is always an indication of what to quit next. With the release of family, I discovered my addiction to life. I was terrified of dying. I was holding to life with my mind, and imposing this addiction on my body. The two had to be separated before they could be reunited. We were back home about three months after the Atlanta trip, when the invitation came. It was the invitation to die. Life, some would think, would be complete with a visitation from Jesus, but it wasn't. I had to quit life. This was a test and an extreme stripping away. Unlike the instantaneous breakthrough in Atlanta, this one took time. I vividly recall my wife cradling my head in her lap as I wept, nearly vomited, and convulsed with diarrhea. For a year and a half, I expected to die the next moment. I was not obsessed with death; that would mean that I had the same thought over and over. Instead, each thought of death was a new thought. Every time it was novel, but always frightening. At times my heart would race, pounding in my chest. I wished for a reprieve, if only I could live another day, but death arrived thousands of times per day. Death can be just thinking more often about death than about life. If disease makes us tender, which it often does, death knocks down all barriers and makes us totally open. Death is not a closing; it is an opening. If you are afraid of death, it is impossible to live. Night after night the agony went on. I dreaded the night.

In a moment of distrust, I went to the doctor. Perhaps there was some medical explanation and cure for what was happening to me. The doctor hooked me up to fancy machines and pronounced me fit. My heart, it seemed, didn't tell the machine that it could stop at any moment; and I wasn't supposed to know that it could. It took that year and a half for my mind to release its hold on my body, for me to release life and death. Death would not excuse me, and my life would not be an excuse for anything. Death brought me to the moment, it removed anything I could take for granted and replaced it with the moment. Death is the end of past and future; death is the moment, and the cultural rule about death is that it is unavoidable. Ironically, in dying so often, in letting go so often, death became impossible, a ridiculous exercise in futility. After a year and a half, the laughter arrived again. One moment I would be shaking in terror, and in the next, laughing uncontrollably. I had not escaped death; I had just died often enough that death finally was irrelevant. I was ready to die and, at the same moment, I was ready to live. My little heart attacks stopped, and now only appear if I need them. If I hold to anything, I get to die again, the blessed letting go.

Q

It didn't feel right to Mary. She shifted her weight, very carefully, but it didn't help. The clay pot on her head had become a part of her. She took it off when she slept, but other than that she and her burden were one. She had come to depend on its weight. Like a small person with a huge helium balloon, she might be in jeopardy of lifting off the ground and floating away without the ballast of her vessel. She did not recognize her dependence, she simply needed it. But this morning there was a problem she had not had yesterday. She had raised the stakes today without knowing it. The vessel was empty, and it wasn't heavy enough for her that way. For years she had been happier when it was full; now she couldn't stand it when it was empty. She no longer even cared what it was filled with, as long as the contents were sufficiently heavy.

As quickly as she could, Mary filled the vessel with water. Yes, that felt better. That was more like it. She had just crossed a point from worthlessness to usefulness. She needed water from the well, but there was nothing that she needed to take to the well. Thus, it follows that she would go to the well with the vessel empty and return with it full. As someone who needed to have it always full, she could not go to the well with it empty. She was way ahead of her time. The cross-country trucker hauls a load each way; he cannot afford to operate for long without the truck filled with something. Mary could take water to the well, then bring water back from the well; what good was that? In her primitive village nobody ever carried anything to the well; that wasn't the purpose of going to the well. She lived in the desert, and water was the most important commodity there was. Her trip to the well was not only her connection with other villagers, but her life and that of her husband and four children depended on her bringing home as much water as she could.

When psychology gets in the way of necessity, there is a problem, one that must be resolved or it could well be the end of the person with the problem, and, in this case, the whole family. Psychology and necessity are not on the same level, but, if one thinks they are, one can justify almost any whim of one's mind. Mary was about to sacrifice her whole family for the sake of her psychological need for a burden. She would have to protect the water in the house from being used so that she would have enough weight to take back to the well. There are probably a number of simple solutions obvious to the reader, but dear reader, remember when you are in the situation yourself, those solutions are not nearly as obvious as they are from the outside. The way this story works is that you can't talk to Mary but Mary can talk to you, so all of your solutions are in vain for her; use them yourself if you are carrying any burdens. One of the things that made Mary's plight particularly difficult is that the people in her village were very easily influenced, and she knew that it would be only a few days until all the people in the village would have the same problem she was having, and would adopt whatever solution she implemented. So she thought she had to multiply the cost of her problem, and the probable cost of any solution, by the fifty families in the village. "What if everyone did that?" was not theoretical here, it was the immediate reality. These people enjoyed their connection to each other, and even thought of themselves as the same person. They cooperated in everything, so a problem was soon everyone's problem. Well, Mary had a problem, a new problem, a problem that she couldn't even be sure was her own, because she might have acquired it from one of the other village dwellers. No problems were ever talked about; they were just spread around, as if in the air. Mary had invented or caught a commitment to burden that did not allow her family to have water that morning. Mary woke first, and the rest of the family awoke within minutes. That is the way it always was. And also the way it always was, is that Mary served the members of the household water and dates. This morning there were dates but no water. She needed the water, so they couldn't have it. The whole family looked at her, not even waiting for the water, because the water and the dates always arrived at the same time. Yet, there were only dates. The couple had been married for eleven years, which was long enough to ingrain the morning date and water pattern in everyone in the house—her husband who had married the pattern, and the four children who had been born into it. The whole family was in trance, staring, blank and empty. The impossible had happened; they could not see the impossible, so they saw nothing at all. I wish you could have seen the situation; it went on and on, with Mary standing there with the full vessel on her head and her family frozen absolutely still like a group of statues. "Woman with the family of statues," was the title of this art piece, the first time Mary had been with her family without any influence from them at all. She was alone, something she had never been before. There was always a family member around; nobody was ever allowed to be alone. An unspoken rule of the village was that alone was impossible; the only way you could exist was with another person or many people.

Mary did the unthinkable for the second time that day as she stood there alone. It seems that she was the first person in the village to think of something other than the circumstances she was in at the moment. She thought of her life before she was married. The clay vessel had been given to her on her wedding day. In her culture it was like a wedding ring. Every time she carried the vessel, it indicated that she was married and that she had come of age. Prior to her marriage, she had seen her mother and the other woman in the town carry their vessels to get water, but she had never carried anything on her head, even in play. Marriage and the vessel were one here, except on this day, because Mary could think of not carrying the vessel and still be married. That is, in fact, what she was doing right now. She still felt the comfort of the weight on her head, but she was thinking of how nice it was when she had not had to carry it everywhere.

For men, it was different. The rites of passage had to do with hunting, which they did occasionally, and that was all. They did not have to carry any burden, and it was no accident that they did not. With perspective, they would have said that it would be impossible to hunt with a burden. Woman were the beasts of burden, and everything rested on their heads, both really and figuratively. Men hunted and killed time until the next hunt; that is the way it had always been. Mary didn't know why it was that way; it just was the way it was. She couldn't question it, because it was all she had known. But in this moment, this moment of being alone, she could think almost anything. What she couldn't do was control her thoughts. In the three hours that this moment lasted, she thought, and thought, and thought. She thought a lifetime of thoughts. She not only imagined a life where she did not have to carry a burden, but a place where men carried the burden, and another place where men and woman shared the burden.

Stretching even farther into the impossible, and removing the vessel from her head, she thought of a place where nobody had to carry a vessel at all, and a place where the water ran in pipes to peoples houses, and they carried imaginary burdens in place of the real vessel with water in it. The thoughts ran on. She thought of foods she had never eaten, of desserts, whatever they were, and of ice. She thought of mangoes, cantaloupe, and airplanes, all things that she would never see in her lifetime and could not explain to anyone. She had dreamed before; but now she was awake, really awake, and dreaming. She had seen mirages many times, but now her thoughts were too real to be mirages. She hardly noticed that the vessel was not in place; her family remained unstirring.

She thought as many thoughts as can occur in several hours, almost infinite, and to her it was. Finally she was done. Mary reached toward the vessel, poured water for each of her family members, and, as she finished pouring the last one, her husband and children returned. It was like they had never gone, for them. For Mary, she would never be the same again. She had thought what cannot be thought. She had adopted different perspectives independent of space and time. She had become a special person in the village, and like special people through the ages, she would be in one of two categories: she would be revered and become a sage, or she would be considered crazy. From here it could go either way, it was up to her, though it didn't do her much good that it was up to her, since she didn't know it.

Like everything, this was taken care of. She reached

down, hoisted the vessel onto her head, and smiled. Yes, she would be a sage. The difference between a sage and a crazy person is that the sage reveals revelations to others at a rate barely faster than they can handle, examine, and kill them; and a crazy person reveals everything all at once. Mary would be a sage. She had put the vessel on, and her smile was like no smile her family had ever seen before. It had a depth, a wisdom beyond what was considered possible; it was unsettling to them, and totally truthful to her. It was just beyond what they could deal with, but not yet quite real enough to put them into trance. Within weeks they were able to adapt to the smile sufficiently that they could return such a smile to her. She became the village teacher, and within two years she was able to remove the vessel without causing too much problem. It took a lot of work, but her husband finally learned to carry water from the well, not on his head but in his arms; it hurt his back a little, but he just carried less water and made more trips. Mary taught the children of the village, and vicariously taught the adults. She taught by example; and everything she taught made the mangoes, cantaloupe, and airplanes more likely.

The day she removed the vessel, never to put it on her head again, was not an important day. On that morning, she had ceased to need her burden with her family, so it was no longer her burden that she was removing. She was unburdened and unburden-able from that day on.

However difficult quitting can be along the way, the reward for continually quitting is enlightenment, well worth any difficulties or problems.

Section Two
A Piece of Cake

Introduction to Cake

However hard it is to quit your job or a relationship, it is just that easy to quit much more subtle games, but only after you have already quit the other ones. There are layers of games in the illusion you call life. Some of them are so gross, they are obvious to you even before you quit anything, though you probably don't call them games. These gross games, such as career, or watching TV, consume much of your waking time and isolate you from life, love, and the successful pursuit of happiness. They do so by making what is least important seem important to you, and keeping you busy in the process. Underlying these gross games are games of such subtlety that they bond you to the philosophies of the cultural prejudices that have you think you are unique, while you are really like everyone else. Examples of these subtle games are the way you go about things: the bizarre idea that you have choice is one of these, as is cause and effect, and stimulus wed to response. To question these before you have quit many other games is impossible, because you can't even see these.

The next few chapters in the Cake Series may appear impossible to see until you have quit many things. I suggest that, before you go on to read the following chapters, you quit many things. Start with things that look small and unimportant, and move on to ones that look big and important. Holding on influences your perspective of their size and importance. As you quit, you will discover the connections between big and small. Also, what once looked small to you may loom large at, or after, the moment you quit it. You just might be surprised that often the things you think would be the hardest to quit are the easiest and vice versa. You also may be surprised, as you speed up, from traveling without all the baggage of presuppositions, rules, and stories you have been carrying, that you are much smarter than you thought you were, and that you are ready to tackle the much more subtle foundations of your dissatisfaction and unhappiness, replacing them with enlightenment and lightness. Quit, then read on.

Cake One

What most people call life is a combination of stories, rules, and presuppositions. None of these have anything to do with existence, except they color your perception of your existence and, thus, they make up the illusion. For example, the icing does not influence the cake, but it does determine your attitude toward the cake and the way you taste it. For some, the icing is the entire reason for eating the cake. Illusion is the icing; existence is the cake.

The process of cutting through the illusion is equivalent to taking apart everything you consider to be true. There are many ways to dismantle the illusion. One is to continually ask yourself both, "What is important?" and "Am I important?" To make these questions useful, it is necessary to frequently provide different answers. At first you may skirt the issue, but soon you will begin to cut through the illusion. Illusion is holographic, in that each part of it appears to be the whole. People defend the illusion by focusing on only part and calling it the whole. The illusion resists cutting. It does so by referring upward; one story refers to another story, which refers to another story, which refers to yet another. Within storyland, it will appear that illusion (the whole structure of presuppositions, rules, and stories) exists. You must get out of the stories entirely, reveal the stories as stories, to cut through them. When you cut through something, you get to what lies underneath it. Hence, what lies underneath stories are the rules that you are run by. Tangled in stories, it is impossible to get to the rules that these stories obscure. And because people spend so much time identifying themselves as their illusion, there is this temptation to stay within the stories.

Since any part can look like the whole, it is sometimes difficult to perceive which is the whole and which is a part resembling the structure. The point at which you can perceive choice reveals what point is the rules, while anything underneath it is presuppositions, and anything above it is stories; in other words, where are you in control of what is or what happens, as opposed to just discovering what is or what happens.

Most people spend their time in the shallowest of illusions. This is where there are only stories that they are defending as truth, and where their stories are perceived as the whole. Within this structure, one perceives the stories as being stories, rules, and presuppositions instead of just stories. They operate as if the stories are the rules and the rules are presuppositions. This misperception allows the rules and presuppositions to be protected by the stories, thus reducing the probability of ever cutting through the illusion to view the rules. These people make little parts of their illusion into the whole by forcing the structure of the whole illusion on any part. This is called a loop. No matter how small, each loop is a game. Within this game, there will always be presuppositions, rules, and stories. The smaller the game, the more repetition it entails. Since repetition is often perceived as safety, a smaller loop is considered the best loop. Is it better to be a big fish in a small pond than a small fish in a big loop? Ask any big fish in a small pond, and you will discover that there is no freedom or ability to move. The big fish may think that he or she is in control, but that control is primarily limitation. A big fish in a small bowl appears to be a captive, while, when people are playing a very small and repetitive game, they consider themselves to be safe. The price they pay for safety is limitation. The fish swims round and round with nothing new to explore or discover, and with only fixed surroundings. People loop around and around a small game, fixing anything that changes so that it stays more the same and they appear safer.

Within a game, staying in the game is the most important rule. A game which has a rule that you can get out of the game is an endangered game. A game must appear mandatory to ensure its own existence.

There is a simple secret to life. Keep reading. The

secret of life will be revealed to you before the end of this chapter.

There is nothing. There is no you, just nothing. Presuppositions initiate mandatory differentiation for your existence. Presuppositions preempt choice by defining one thing from everything else. The choice of one thing from everything is too painful and difficult for you to make, so you pretend that it isn't you making it. You say that it exists and thus there is no choice. However, if you could perceive at this level, as opposed to the level of stories where you spend almost all of your time, you would be able to choose existence. You would be able to create yourself from nothing and still know that you are nothing. Yet, presuppositions preempt that; thus, you have to be something. Otherwise, you would be absolutely free. Presuppositions restrict being by determining being. They restrict the perception of the whole to certain expressions, and they are entirely invented.

Moving to rules from presuppositions crosses the lines of judgment; it transports existence into the world of good-bad, right-wrong. At first, rules draw a line down the middle and attempt to control choice at this level. Anything from one side of the line is good and anything from the other is bad—it's black or white. The choice in rules is only between two things, at least at first. Soon there are enough rules that the initial line becomes distorted into many lines and people become gray.

Rules determine preferences, and attempt to limit thinking. If rules are all important, then thinking is unimportant. Rules are there not only to limit what you think, but even the necessity to think. You do not have to figure out how fast you will drive down the road; all you need to do is look at the speed limit sign and have your speedometer match the sign. There may be consequences for not obeying the sign. Here, people go from a rule about speed back to the original rule of good and bad; it is good to obey the sign. Rules eliminate personal responsibility by giving a person an acceptable range of behaviors. At the level of rules, our choices are perceived through the filter of which rules will be followed and which will not.

People will depend on rules but they don't like them, so they invent stories to justify following or not following the rules. In stories, choice is preempted with cause and effect. People do things for reasons; so the reasons determine what they do, rather than themselves. Again, people are evading personal responsibility. Every story justifies and/or excuses something, thus hiding the rules and presuppositions. Stories are manifested from a very limited perspective, one in which you are able to control.

Where you are perceiving, whether it be at the level of stories, rules, or presuppositions, determines your possible quality of life. At the level of stories, other people do not exist; only the fabrications are perceived as true. You mistake the part for the whole, just because the part resembles the whole. And the part only resembles the whole because it is you looking at it. At the level of rules, you think you have a choice of what story to tell, and are directed by the rules. Here, rules will become your presuppositions, thus you will be either a good or a bad person. Rules throw you into a world of other people, while stories take you away from that world into a personal iso-lated world, i.e., the only world where you could con-ceive that you create your own reality. If you perceive that you have a choice about what rules you follow, and what ones you don't, then your existence is not in doubt, and your thinking becomes important. You look at the rules, rather than just what you have created. Most rules are cre-ated by other people and followed by you. The very act of looking at the rules brings your attention to your relation-ship with other people. At the level of presuppositions, you can perceive rules, and even their existence, as op-tional. Here you can choose to exist or not. You can no longer be good or bad; you just are. You face death as an offer not to exist. Moving choice to before presupposi-tions has choice disappear, because the basis of choice is differentiation. So, prior to the level of presupposition, there is no difference, only unity and wholeness.

The first rung of the ladder out of the Garden of Eden is presupposition, the second is rules, and the third is sto-ries. As you reach the third rung, the garden is long since forgotten, and all life is a metaphor. People have sepa-rated themselves from everything, making it impossible to recognize who they are as the whole. From here, reading a book or watching a movie is no longer any different from life. You think that wherever you are is the whole, thus think you are in the garden. The ladder gets shaky up this high. The position is precarious, and precarious is bad. As you tell more stories and think they are true, you be-come more and more top heavy. You hold to the rung, you depend on the rung, and you don't dare look down. Look up, that will put things in perspective. You shake, you are scared, the ladder shakes too. The more it shakes, the tighter you hold.

Never underestimate the power of a story to delude or entertain you. Illusions can have your next kiss be your first kiss while reality can have your current kiss be your only kiss. Illusions can take you back to the time you were walking home from the big dance with a girl or a boy by your side, the nervousness as you turned and touched your lips to his, losing the presence of mind, feeling the body, a body not your own, touching yours. The warmth, the softness, the newness, and the nervousness were all part of that moment; and they can again be a part of kissing your spouse after fifty years of marriage. Illusions can lead you to the most exciting wonderful places. They can provide you with constant entertainment.

Delusion is thinking that illusion is true and leads you to craziness. Where you perceive choice to be, based on how much you must justify, determines whether your stories are true for you, are delusions, or are created by you (illusions).

When you consider a story to be true, it will always conflict with rules and presuppositions sufficiently to lock you into that story. This may be perceived as a hellacious loop that forms around your delusions. The game is to keep in place whatever you perceive to be true, with you as the sentry constantly dizzy circling and keeping guard. The less you consider to be true, the smaller your loop, and the smaller your game. As you become less deluded, and your game becomes smaller, you move toward the level of presuppositions, where you are predifferentiation. For about the first two years, a child is part of the whole and isn't yet able to perceive a separation. At about two or three years of age (when consciousness arrives), the child starts to perceive its own existence. As children seek more, they encounter rules. The child is allowed to do this but not that. Allowed to eat this but not that. Allowed to go here but not there. The rules begin to obscure existence and to distract. The child's thinking is coerced into focusing on learning the rules, rather than just learning. Later on, the child learns that it is acceptable to break some rules if there are stories that justify breaking those rules. The child is led up the ladder, out of the Eden that he or she was born into.

The secret to life is always perceiving that you have a choice and never taking it. If you perceive that you have no choice, you are stuck. If you perceive that you have a choice, then there is the constant temptation to make it. If you make the choice, you will then have to justify it forever. Adam and Eve and the apple; they could choose it or not. The rule was that they were not to eat it. They were tempted, made the choice, and were doomed forever.

Your thinking is never more open and vital than when you perceive that you have an important choice and have not yet made the choice. At that balancing point, your senses are piqued. The moment you make the choice, you have lost every option but one and you are doomed to focus on that one. You have split the world, and you must learn to live and defend that tiny little part of the world you have chosen. The fall is choosing; you fall up the ladder and leave paradise behind. You define yourself by the choice, and the less important the choice, the less important you become. The secret, again, is always perceiving that you have a choice and never making it.

The moment that you make a choice, the game begins. Quitting is returning yourself to before choice. Pretend that you believe in Adam and Eve and the apple; do you really have to keep paying for Adam's bite? You don't have to, and the way that you can turn back the clock is to not bite yourself. If you don't bite, then you don't choose, and you don't get caught up in the game. You don't make what isn't more important than what is, and you are constantly open; you are the whole. The way that you escape perception of the whole is through choice. The level at which you perceive that you are making the choice determines how small a game you are playing, and the rewards of any game are comparable with its size. The bigger the game, the bigger the reward. Having no game at all reveals you as big as you can get and gives you everything— total expansion. The smallest game will always look like the whole, as will all other games. Quitting a small game will always give you a bigger game. Quitting the biggest game will give you the whole. You already have the whole, but the quitting of the biggest game will unite you with what you perceive and what is. At that moment you are whole and you know it. This is the end of all games and what life was like before the games. The circle is complete and everything is within it. There is no repetition within the whole, because all the smaller games/loops disappear and there is only one loop/game. The smaller the game, the more repetition. Lose interest in all repetition, and you will discover yourself quitting.

Always perceive that you have a choice, and never make it; that is quitting before you start. Quitting any game only requires perceiving, rather than making choices. As you perceive them, choices reveal themselves as larger and larger. As you don't choose, your range of choices increases. Life becomes expansive rather than limiting. As you continually don't choose, you will discover that you have free time, time that you are not forced to choose. Your life will open and you can play in the moment, the only time there is to play. You can work anytime, all you have to do to work is make a choice. Choice is the manifestation of control. If you don't control, then you can include; if you do control, then you must rule. What you can rule is so little that your game will be small. If you do not need to control, and even seek not to control, then your game will expand. You will have less repetition and more novelty. You will discover yourself over and over again. You will love what you see, and you will see what you love. You will laugh, cry, and not be able to tell the difference because there is no difference. If there was a difference between the two, you would have to prefer one over the other, and then you would have to justify your preference until you defined yourself by that preference. Thus, you would have done another loop. If you don't choose you don't loop, and there are no games, but one.

Cake Two

I am the chosen one. I have been chosen for my role very carefully, and I really am the chosen one.

You, too, are the chosen one. If you could stop trying to prove that you were the chosen one, you would discover that you are. If you could get off the roller coaster long enough that your busyness and addiction to externally created speed disappeared, or abated somewhat, you would be in a position to perceive just how wonderful you are. However, almost everyone is stuck within an artificial continuum, and they're trying to prove where they stand on that continuum. Yet, things that are "the case" don't need to be proven. People go on trying, though, to prove how good or how bad they are not, that they can do something well, or never do something else. A fundamental element of this proving is choice. It is you who chooses something over something else. It is you who guides your life in the direction it is going. It is you who chooses the games you are playing and goes on choosing those games.

Or isn't it?

The moment you perceive that you have made a choice, any choice, no matter how big or small, you forfeit your role as the chosen one and become the chooser instead. You give up your connection with everything, and make more important your connection with something in particular. While this specialization seems to make you a friend, with whatever you chose, it, at the same moment, alienates you from everything else in the universe and cements your place in illusion. Free choice is anything but free. Free choice has something appear to be you that isn't. The moment you choose, you lose your omnipotence and isolate yourself from so much. Choice is one of the initial building blocks of illusion. Making a choice has you dislike who you perceive yourself to be, since it alienates you so thoroughly from who you are. The mouse may claim that it is the most important creature on the planet, and that its little cheese chase is all that matters, but that does not make it so. A mouse is too smart to make such a claim, though; are you? Once you have chosen, you have so much more to choose, so much to support and prove, that one choice leads you into a lifetime of supporting (proving) that choice. Choice turns life sour, while seemingly setting it free. There is no choice. If you could go several minutes without making a choice, you would realize your enlightenment, connect with everything, and be free. You would discover that you are the universe, not the one who has been appointed to tame the universe. Freedom is another word for having everything. But, to have everything, you must be everything; and to be everything, you must be nothing; and that gets you back to the roots that nourish you.

A very important thing to quit is choice. Like all other quitting, you can continue to see it, but you must stop throwing your weight behind one fork or another of the choice. As long as you continue to perceive yourself as a chooser, you will get hooked by what you choose and have to defend your perceived choice. There is no real choice; you always get everything, thus you are giving up only illusion. Career is much easier to quit than choice, so is television or parenting. Balanced at the point of a perceived choice, all difference lies to you from your perception. Choice beckons this way, or that or some other way. "Or" is the key word here, because, when you perceive that you have made a choice, you have lost the whole; you have settled for some instead of everything, and, in that same moment, you have differentiated yourself as the chooser. Identity quickly follows, with all of its opinions about what should be chosen, and then follows justifications for every choice.

Adam was obsessed by the apple. That there was something he could not have, made his life miserable. The moment he perceived he could have *something,* everything but that thing looked empty. He had to have the forbidden fruit. The produce section in paradise contained all sorts of fruit, perfectly ripe and succulent fruit in abundance. There were mangoes and passion fruit, papaya and kiwi, oranges and pineapples. The most exotic and commonplace fruits in absolute abundance, but Adam could only perceive the apple. He could and did look past everything to that one thing. He made a choice, the first choice which led you right to where you are. Worse yet, he set it up so that he could blame his choice on Eve, a blame which, spoken or not, continues to the present day.

When he perceived the apple to the exclusion of everything else, paradise disappeared. He lost all the other fruit. The morning before the fall, he had a papaya and two mangoes for breakfast, along with bacon and eggs. The morning he became the chooser, all he could have was an apple. The universe shrunk and, most importantly, at that moment, Adam's perspective of himself shrunk. What would you think of someone who, confronted with everything, chose one small thing? Worse yet, chose that small thing not because he or she wanted it, but because they were not allowed to have it? From that moment on, low self-esteem ruled. Stupidity entered the world. I certainly hope that it was a tasty wonderful apple, since all that happened after it is so rotten.

Quitting free choice is easy, once you can see that there is no free choice anyway. People keep free choice around to keep themselves importantly unimportant. If you really were important, you wouldn't need free choice to prove it. You could be in paradise again. Paradise revisited is as wonderful as it ever was. You can be the chosen one. When you don't chose, you will discover that you are the chosen one, always were, and always will be. The only thing that you can lose, quit, is illusion. One of the wonderful things about quitting is that it is safe. You can only quit what doesn't exist. Thus, you lose nothing and, paradoxically, gain nothing as you quit. Wait, don't make that choice. If you do, you will have the whole universe come down on you, around you. You will suffocate trying to prove that who you think you are is who you are, while everything else in the universe is indicating that you are not who you perceive yourself to be. Let choice go free, let choice be and it will let you be.

You have to know where you stand to make a choice, but you have to make a choice to know where you stand. Caught in this bind, backed into this corner, you must fight for your freedom, and if you are fighting, you are not free.

Cake Three

Who decides what you eat? It is decided in the rules section of life. Not just what you eat is decided, but also whom you eat with, where you eat, what you do, and almost every aspect of how you live. The few exceptions are not worth noting. You don't even decide when to breathe. You almost always breathe automatically, and your breathing is determined outside of your consciousness by the people around you. Every breath you take in the presence of others is influenced by the way the people around you are breathing. Spend some time around someone asthmatic if you don't think that this is the case. Anything outside of your awareness is deeply influenced by your surroundings. To consciousness, it seems it only accepts the existence of what it can perceive. So, the subtlety of this influence continually escapes consciousness, with a few notable exceptions such as God.

Imagine that you are twenty-five years old and female. You are considered good looking and have an attractive body. Are you going to have children? This is an important question; ask anyone who has children and they will confirm that life with children is very different from life before children. The cultural pressure to have children is great; not as great as it was twenty or fifty years ago, but still there is pressure. Nobody lives in a vacuum; they just suffocate there. So our fictitious female must decide whether or not to have children. It is likely that her parents have opinions regarding her choice to have children or not, her friends have opinions, her brothers and sisters have opinions, the TV shows she watches illustrate rules about having kids. Her employment status, her living quarters, her preferences for how she likes to spend her time, and her entire history with men may influence her decision. In short, there are so many influences that come to bear that she cannot just decide whether she wants to have children. She must think long and hard, factoring in so much that is outside of her, but still influencing her. It doesn't seem fair to factor in all these influences when it is she and the children who will have to live intimately with her decision.

She never really gets to decide whether or not to have children. I am not supposed to say that, but she doesn't decide. The circumstances, well beyond her control, decide. Pure choice comes from nothing, not from a lot of somethings. Influence comes from the somethings, all the input outside of herself. Who she really is is nothing, and, if she could get back to that even for a moment, she could make a perfect choice. The weighing in of the different variables is a confusing mess at best; it puts unbearable pressure on her. Almost everyone will say that she should have the right to choose, but nobody is willing to notice that that right has been preempted. It is not her that will choose. The choice will be made for her, and she will think that she has made the choice. One of the rules in this democracy is that she has to think that she made the choice herself. So she does.

She is the most intimately connected to the choice; however, she doesn't get to make it. The sum total of all input surrounding any choice is culture. All that has pre-ceded the choice influences which way the choice goes. Culture leans over her shoulder and tells her to have a child, or not. Fifty years ago, culture told her she had to have a child; today, it says that it is acceptable for her to wait for a few years before she has children, but she still had better have children at some point. In the South, the age for having children is earlier than it is in the Midwest. Examining the age that most woman become mothers for the first time in different sections of the country will re-veal the varying amounts of cultural pressure.

Culture is a mixture of rules perpetrated upon each individual by all individuals. Culture advocates you tak-ing a bite out of a specific part of the universe, and then it is you who must chew it and derive nourishment from it. Culture says to the thirty-five-year-old married woman that she must have children soon or she will miss her chance. Culture is relentless; it has been saying versions of the same thing to her now for at least ten years. She stalled it off this long, but now she is invited again. The cultural influence is too much for the individual; it is too persistent to be thwarted, and thus she gets pregnant and has a child. She now must play the parenting game.

Culture, the set of rules, inspired the birth of the child, pushed the young mother-to-be into a specific game, parenting. It said to take that bite, identify yourself, play that game. Parenthood is one example of a culturally forced game, but there are many. In fact, culture has rules regarding any game you wish to play, and input about your very act of wishing. It is likely that you never do anything that is not determined by culture. Anytime that you go the least bit against culture, the people around you rise in resistance. They tell you why you can't or shouldn't do that which you are contemplating. They let you know the consequences, they speak their part, play the mouthpiece of culture and say what they are supposed to say. While they are speaking, they think they are uttering their own opinions, and attempting to help you at the same time. Almost everyone is a cultural law enforcer. Having a job is a rule enforced by culture. *You must get married, you must get divorced, you must retire, you must go on vacation, you must send your children to school, you must watch TV, you must read the bestsellers, and you must know what is happening in the world.* These are all rules of our culture, and they are enforced aggressively. The people who ask the young couple when they are getting married may appear to be engaging in small talk; but when the same question is asked over and over by different people, the nature of culture reveals itself. Cultural rules are always enforced. They can be broken, but there will be a loss. The loss will be some of what you have in common with everyone else.

Remember that culture is a group of rules. Culture changes over time, and there are smaller cultures within bigger cultures. There are cultures which go cross-culture. If our young woman had been a member of the Catholic culture, and had broken a rule about having sex, she would have encountered the rule that she must have the child. An Eskimo lends his wife for the night as a token of friendship, while an Italian will supposedly kill anyone who sleeps with his wife. These are cultural rules, acted out by individuals who often think the rules are their own. People carry the rules, but the rules act through them. People congregate together by the rules they follow. The Mennonites have certain rules, the Amish others, and the people who work for IBM yet others. Rules produce identities; they define not only what people do and don't do, but also who people perceive themselves to be.

Living out the dictates of culture precludes individual existence. It eliminates choice, but not the perception of choice. People within a culture perceive that they can make different choices, but they almost always make the same ones. Personal responsibility cannot exist without the individual; so in culturally defined games, it does not exist. Even though it doesn't exist, it is still considered to exist; after all, it is the foundation of our country. The typical result of culture preempting choice is that the person disappears and culture triumphs. At any point that the person attempts to go against a cultural rule, there are multiple invitations not to.

The individual him or herself is distracted by the red herring of personal responsibility, and thus must think and think and think about the consequences of each choice or decision. Each individual must carry the weight of the choice upon themselves. Like a great magician, culture does the trick. Culture makes the decision and distracts the audience, in this case the person who thinks he or she is deciding, from noticing what is really going on. It isn't until later that the person who has made the choice gets tired of living with the choice and needs someone to blame for the choice. At three in the morning, the new mother gets up with her one-year-old and wonders why she ever had a child in the first place. She isn't supposed to wonder that, so she stops. Just like she wasn't supposed to breast feed past six months, and was supposed to give her child a pacifier.

Culture has rules for everything; and anytime the new mom comes up for air to ponder whether she really wants this game, she discovers that she has signed up for a lifetime of parenthood and that the contract is binding. She can blame anyone for her being a parent because everyone had a hand in it. She can blame the father, the baby, her parents, her friends, the TV shows, her religion, and herself. She has a legitimate complaint against anyone in the culture who directed her to be in this position. If she caves in to the temptation, she again misses that it is the culture which directed her and preempted her choice. Rules are there to follow, and it is not the specific person who is carrying the rules who is to blame; if they put the rules down, someone else would pick them up.

People don't pick their friends, rules pick their friends. The games they are engaged in pick their friends. People are around certain people because they have something in common with them; all that people can have in common are presuppositions, rules, or stories. Presuppositions are perceived by so few people that they don't determine people's friends. Stories determine superficial friendships (friendships which can be justified), and rules determine who can be allowed to be a friend and who can't. You can have a relationship in which you argue, but you must at least have common rules about what is allowed in the argument. It is the rules, culture, which determines our friends. Culture is a group of people with common rules. You are friends with whom you should be friends, and you are not friends with whom you should not be friends. If you are friends with someone just because you want them to purchase something from you, that is a friendship based on stories, and it goes no deeper than the story. Marriage is an attempt to define and enforce a specific set of rules between two people. Parenting is another. Fifty years ago, marriage required people of different sexes; today, there are states that allow people of the same sex to get married. Culture grudgingly adapts to allow such changes. Anyone who is outside the culture will be discriminated against. Fifty years ago, homosexuality was nearly imperceptible; today, it is obvious. Perception by a culture is a step on the way to acceptance by that culture. What people can just barely see today may be a part of the culture in the future.

As soon as five people are playing the same game, a culture arises. The rules fight for their own existence, their own importance, and they get carried by someone. The more people who are playing a game, the stronger the culture. By being born into a culture, you are born into specific rules. Your acceptance or rejection of these rules will define much of your life. Your inability to perceive the rules will have you think that the rules are presuppositions, just the way things are. The more games you are involved in, the more rules you must follow, if not observe. Any game that you cannot observe as rules will direct you unseen. If you see and question the rules, then you will open the possibility of abiding by the rules or not. This opening creates room for freedom and pure choice. Cultural rules can be broken, but they still continue to influence all aspects of anyone's life within the culture. Any quitting that you do offends culture.

Republican | Intellectual
Dog Owner | Card Player
Husband | Catholic
A Man | Cake Four | Middle Aged
Overweight | Angry
Irish | Tall

Each of the above labels requires that you perform certain functions and obey specific rules, or pay a price for disobeying them. All of the games you play work together to define who you are, to form an identity. They determine both what you do and what you can perceive. There is an order of importance that these games are in; and that order determines, to some degree, your priority of rules. As a man, you may well want to make love to many women, but as a Catholic and a husband, you may not be able to. As a husband, you need to provide for your family, but you also need to spend time with them. The computer programmer in you has little interest in family. During football season, the TV becomes more attractive than your wife. As a dog owner, you must continually balance your interest in your dog with your other duties. The combination of games you play determine all that you will do with your life, and almost all you will think. The built-in rules of each game will define your playing field, and the hierarchy of rules will determine the unique individual that you are. The husband and father and man in you may have compassion for the street person, but the Republican may think that the street person should get up, brush themselves off, and get a job. On any subject, on any day, you will have something to say. This conglomeration of games you call yourself defines your life. To you, it is you.

But it really isn't you. It has nothing to do with you. It is who you have called yourself. You react to the different games; you know some of the rules of each game, and seek to obey them while keeping your priorities straight. If you have an affair, then your Catholic game suffers a bit, as does your husband game. When there is a big project at work, all the games except computer programmer may temporarily diminish in importance. You may discover at work that you get attention you never get at home, and soon you are spending more and more time at work. All of the other games become less important than work. The more games you are playing, the greater the balancing act you must perform, and the more you must become a negotiator attempting to keep the peace between all of the parts of you that make up your identity.

The likelihood that you will perceive most of the rules in any game is small. The likelihood that you will perceive all of the rules is about zero. Any rule you don't perceive has its way with you. With the rules that you can perceive, you judge how good or bad you are by your adherence to them. If you think that you should spend a lot of time with your children, but you don't, then you think that you are not a very good daddy. The Catholic church requires tithing; if you don't give the money that you should, you are nagged by breaking that rule. If you lust after women other than your wife, you are not as good a husband as you should be. If being a good pet owner requires your going out for walks with the dog, you can become a lousy pet owner by attending to the story that you are too tired to take a walk with the dog. You individualize the game by obeying or disobeying rules. Rules that you don't perceive become presuppositions for you; they become who you are.

It doesn't matter how well you play; all of the rules of a game still apply. As long as you are playing the game, you will have rules that you must abide by. The way to avoid rules, and not be torn apart by them, is to quit the game. As long as you keep the games in place, you will be busy, so busy that many of the games will be at war and you will become a casualty. You won't have to think much, because rules preempt thinking, but you will have to come up with stories that balance out all of the games you are caught up in. You will play none of the games very well, because you are too busy playing so many games. Your play in individual games will be influenced by all other games, and you will discover that there is not enough time to play all of them well. You will become mediocre, deriving little satisfaction within the balancing act. No matter how much time you spend with your wife on one day, you are still pulled in many other directions the next. Any game you do not attend to suffers, while the game you are attending to consumes your time. There is no possibility of winning in a life composed of so many games.

Life becomes hollow and shallow as you seek to balance all the games. There is a constant offer to take on more games. There is a school board election coming up; you know you really should be on the school board. The church needs your help with a few projects, and your wife needs some time away from the kids. All the games vie for all of your attention. Oh, to have life be simple again. You long for a time when you were not fully defined and ruled, when games did not fill all of your time. Spontaneity has disappeared, as has the love of your spouse. You are lonely, but at least you are busy. In an attempt to be good, you want to give equal time to all games. You love your dog, so you must take care of your dog. After all, part of who you are is a dog owner.

You never have any free time, thus you are not free. If you were free, you would be out of the games for a moment and be able to look at them. You would discover your slavery and fight to be free. You might well try to get your life back, wrestle it from the games that control you, define you.

On Sunday, you turn on the TV set. You know that the dog needs a walk, and that your wife would like a little time with you; but after all, you did work long hours all week, and you did go to Mass this morning. Your favorite team is playing, and you have a big bag of corn chips and a beer. You know that you shouldn't drink the beer or eat the corn chips, but you deserve it don't you? Who decides if you deserve it? What stories must you tell to deserve anything? The story about working hard and going to Mass suffice today to justify football watching and drinking and eating. As you sit down, the phone rings. You know that your spouse is busy so, if you were really good, you would answer the phone, but you don't want to. Again, you are torn by rules. There is a rule that you have as a phone owner that you must answer your phone. Perhaps there is an emergency at work; the computers are down and only you can fix the problem. Perhaps it is your neighbor letting you know that your dog has escaped from your fenced yard and is scaring his children. Perhaps it is your priest wanting to pay you a visit, or your friend Bill wanting to talk to you about his family problems. Perhaps it is a wrong number. All of the games you are engaged in fight for center stage, fight to be your most important game. These games don't have lives of their own; your life is their life.

You ignore the phone and watch the game. You watch people running around on the screen. These people, at least at the moment, are your idols. These are people who live and breathe one game so totally that they have become good, really good, at that game. They are playing football for you because you can't. You enjoy the game as a vicarious participant. You don't care if the quarterback beats his wife and the linebacker does drugs between plays. You are watching them because they are good at one game; they have excluded enough other games that they have become this good at one. You love football. You know the rules of this game. You know where people are allowed to run and where they are not, when they are allowed to hit

Quitting

each other and when they are not. The game is simple
enough that you can think that you understand it. If only
your own life was that simple. If only you could have the
time to devote to what you really want to do. The phone
rings again. Perhaps it is your mother wondering why you
have not called this week (the son game). Or, it might be
someone wanting you to switch phone companies (the
phone-owner game). It might even be somebody from high
school whom you have not spoken to in twenty or thirty
years, calling about your reunion (you probably thought
you were done with the high school game). Memories of
high school flood your mind. Those were the days. You
forget to watch the game and miss a touchdown. Your rev-
erie is interrupted by the cheers from the TV, and you watch
the instant replay. If only there were an instant replay in
life. If only you could have both all that you are missing
and all that you have. The moment you have something, the
moment you do something, you don't have or don't do something else. You can't have it all, not as long as you have
something. Anything that you do have is a constant reminder
of your limitations. Any game you are attending to is a
reminder that you're not attending to other games. There is
too much to do and too little time. There are too many
rules and not enough freedom. You can either think about
high school or watch the game; you can't do both.

You ignore the screen and think of your first love. You
were a sophomore and she was a freshman. You had some
school work to do, but you had your priorities and thinking about her was at the top of the list. You thought of her
no matter what you were doing. When you were in class

you thought of her; when you were at home you thought of her. She was your main game, and, the more you thought of her, the better you liked her. There were few rules to this game, and almost no expectations. You did not want to marry her; you just wanted to think about her. You were free, and into that freedom came an angel. Those were the days, some of the best days of your life. Realizing that the woman in the other room, the woman who is now your wife, is that same girl from high school seems impossible. It is impossible; she is the same person but not really. She is different and you are different. You and she are both involved in so many games, working for so many masters, obeying so many rules and balancing so many responsibilities, that you are no longer free to be in love. Love is inclusion, and there is no room in your life to include anything else. Before you know it the game is over—the football game. You are forced to quit watching because the game is over. You deserved to watch football but you didn't watch much. Even on your day off, even when you could supposedly do what you wanted, the games would not leave you alone. Your beer is empty, as is the corn chip bag, but you don't remember drinking or eating.

What game will you play next? What rules will jump up at you? Within the interlocking balancing act of all of these games, there is only reaction. You react to whatever game appears in the moment. You do not create anything, because creation requires that you start from nothing. You bounce from one game to another. If only you could quit one game, then you would be pulled in fewer directions. You would be less schizophrenic. When you quit a game, you no longer have to obey any of the rules of that game, and you lose all of the stories that justified your following or not following those rules. You discover you are not who you thought you were. Ironically, you find out you are less than you thought you were, and less is somehow more. When you have so many games running, the most you can find out is who you can't be. You find out who you are (identity) from the web of rules that you are unaware of but influenced by. You find out who you can be when you are free enough from rules. As you react to rules, the reactions outline a certain profile that has nothing to do with you. This profile is a busy two-dimensional image that arises from all of the games, but it seems to be all that you have. The more you quit, the less refined and stagnant the image becomes, and the more possibilities you become aware of.

At first a game is so innocent; you watch a new TV show. Soon it becomes very demanding; you can't miss the show, and are telling other people at work that they must watch it too. Watching the first show was optional, and you really enjoyed it, but soon it became mandatory and you had to watch it. Enjoyment disappeared. To be free of the games, you must discover that they are optional. To be oppressed by them, you must consider them to be mandatory. Mandatory games no longer look like games; they look like life and work. They require struggle, balancing, effort, compromise, competition, and comparison. Optional games require nothing. The conversion of optional games to mandatory games occurs when you define yourself by the game, when your life becomes dependent upon the game.

Becoming aware of the rules allows you to see them as rules. This process disengages the stimulus→response mechanism inherent in mandatory games. Converting mandatory to optional goes contrary to the forces of culture, and allows room to explore even more rules. This exploration leads to freedom. You become stimulus→responsible instead of stimulus→response. Free rather than preprocessed and automatic.

Cake Five

New games are continually offered, but there is a limited number of games you can play and still maintain any balance at all. Stress is the likely result of having too many games or too few games. The more that your games look optional, the more flexibility you will have. The more games that you perceive to be mandatory, the stiffer, busier, and crazier you will be. When a game is perceived as optional, the pleasure derived from that game increases. Mandatory games are a bit like medicine that you must take in order to get well; if you don't play the mandatory game, there will be consequences that you don't want to face.

One of two responses is likely to a game that is perceived as mandatory—rebellion or oppression. Rebellion occurs when you are resisting the game. This resistance does not mean quitting; it just means disliking what one is doing, and often refusing to see the game as mandatory while still playing the game. Resisting the game results in a preponderance of stories. These stories deny the necessity of the game, and even attempt to create the impression that the game is not mandatory while behaviors indicate otherwise. The person with a cigarette in hand saying, "I could quit any time I want to, I just don't want to," is an example of stories modifying perceptions. Some people work in the same job for forty years, claiming all the while that the job is temporary, that they can quit any time they want, and soon they will get on with what they really want to do. There comes a time in the life of an aging elevator operator or waitress, when the evidence that the acting career is not going to come about, that denial finally ends. "What do you do?" "I am an actor, waiting tables until my big break comes," says the sixty-five-year-old waitress. Rebellion is resistance to what is while focusing on what could be. Sounds a lot like the definition of a game doesn't it? Rebellion is a game of games. It modifies the perception of games, while holding one as more important or better than another. The game that is not being played is always better, and the game that is being played is always resisted.

Oppression is another game of games. It is a way of organizing games and avoiding responsibility for the games that are currently being played. Oppression is excusing the fact that you are perceiving a game as mandatory by blaming someone else for it being mandatory. I don't want to play this game but I have to because.... What comes next is a story. The story is one that is told often. I am only doing this because of the money, my husband, the children, the government, or my parents. Oppression is unlike rebellion, in that it does not deny the game but rather excuses it with stories. A mother will often blame her children for making her a mother, or a husband will blame his spouse for making him a husband. The husband fantasizes, creates stories, about how wonderful life would be without his wife. If he were only single again, things would be different. They were not different before he met his wife, but stories do not need to be non-fiction; stories just need to justify.

So there are slaves that deny they are slaves, and there are slaves who think that someone or something else made them slaves. In the case of rebellion, all personal exploration and perception must begin and end with stories. Rebellion is an attempt to totally obscure rules. Oppression is telling stories about the rules, and using those rules to prove that the oppressed person is good while the oppressor is bad. Oppression uses the rules, while rebellion seeks to detract attention from them. A dream world full of delusion, distrust, and anger is often the result of rebellion, while oppression usually results in depression or disease. In both cases, quitting does not seem to be a possibility. Rebellion makes quitting impossible, because you can't quit what you have not admitted that you are playing. Oppression preempts quitting, because it is someone else's fault that the game is being played. A combination of these two results in blaming someone else for not quitting a game that you won't even admit you are playing.

Both rebellion and oppression are encouraged, because both keep the games intact. Resisting the game proves what is "real," while blaming someone else for the game makes exploring the game impossible. If the oppressed person examines the game, he or she may discover that the oppression is just a story to justify the game. Anything that avoids quitting is to be rewarded. Win or lose, as long as you are *playing,* the games are all that really matters.

Ironically, as you begin quitting games, you discover that they were never mandatory or real at all. You discover that there is nothing to resist or to justify. Nobody is to blame for illusion. Cutting through the stories will reveal the rules; and examining the rules will uncover the presuppositions, and the games will fall apart. You will no longer need to loop once more around the game. As long as stories are in place, the game cannot be examined. As you dismantle stories, watch for rebellion and oppression. If you think you are working for the money, pretend that you have unlimited money. What would you do then? Take away your own stories, and you will discover that stories are never true, though they distract people from what is really happening. Notice what you are resisting, and then look closely at what is really happening around you. If your job is wonderful and fun, you probably don't have many stories for why you continue to do it. "Would you do your job even if you were not being paid?" As you observe your stories, rather than telling them, you will discover what they hide. What common elements are there in your stories? How often does your spouse serve as a justification for what you would or would not do? How often does money show up as a justification? How often does the way you were raised show up as a justification? How often do other people or the government justify what you would or would not do? Discovering the common themes in your stories will assist you in revealing them as stories, and will lead you to the rules. Soon you will catch yourself before you tell a story, as you realize that there is nothing to justify. Quit justifying, and you will discover a world of rules that determines all that you do and most of what you think.

The more justification you have, the more difficult your life is; it is hard to tell whether the justification came first or afterward. One thing is for certain, the more that you have to excuse, the more excuses you will have, and the worse your life will be. Stories are like notes from your mother; they excuse you from personal responsibility. You learn early in life that if you have a good story you can get away with just about anything. Stories that are not perceived as stories lead you to the most superficial and empty life you can have.

Stories created can be highly entertaining, but stories believed are always misleading and abusive. Stories told in justification lead you away from yourself. They result in the shrinking of the size of the games you can play and require defense. Stories are what you think about what might be. Perception is what you see, hear, or feel.

People live in an additive culture where one of the main rules is that more is better. The more money you have the better, the more you have to do the better, the more stories you have the better, the more rules you have the better, the more freedom that you perceive you have the better. Possessions possess you, and soon you are entirely possessed; there is no you other than the group of games that you are currently locked into. The idea of quitting flies in the face of "more is better." It paradoxically suggests that less is more. So, the more you quit, the fewer games you are playing, the more of you there will be, and the more all-encompassing you will become. Your limitations will fall by the wayside, as will games that you no longer play, stories you don't need to tell, and rules that you don't need to breathe life into. You will discover that you are much more competent than you thought you were.

Appearance replaces substance, since there is no substance to stories. You are less interested in what you did than why you did it. You move farther away from who you are to explain what you did. There is no end to the stories that can be told, as long as you continue to tell stories. As you stop telling stories, and begin to examine the stories you have told, you will discover that there is nothing that needs to be justified, and who you are is fundamentally different from your stories. Certainly you are a story teller, you are able to tell stories, but you do not have to believe the stories you tell.

I have noticed the rule that stories must be true in order to be told. Lying in bed with my children at night, and telling a story that is created in the moment, is lying without lying. All of your stories are created, made up. Telling a story many times, or many people telling a story, does not make it true. It makes it appear to be a rule. The mind will not tolerate such repetition, so it stops telling the obvious stories and just assumes that a story told often enough or by enough people is a presupposition. Thus, repetition legitimatizes stories; that is the whole idea behind a democracy. If enough people are deluded, it is easier to be deluded than not. Truth is not a numbers game, and trust has nothing to do with truth. Stories are always made up and never true. All stories attempt to justify, to hook at least two things together, to force a connection that does not occur naturally. If something were really true, it would not need a story to make it true. Craziness needs a lot of stories. Anytime you have something to hide, believing that a story is true is one of the most efficient ways to hide it. Trust a story teller who knows that he or she is making it up, or just repeating the stories, but never trust one who thinks that the stories are true.

The idea that there are true stories and untrue stories is an attempt to legitimatize illusion, to convert illusion to reality, to have the little bit that people can perceive appear to be all there is. People who think the "right" things are true are worshipped or revered, and institutions are named after them, while people who think the "wrong" things are true are institutionalized.

Stories told for entertainment do not attempt to legitimatize illusion, but ones told for justification do. As you examine your stories, notice particularly those that you know are true. Notice which stories are your stories alone, and which stories only require you to read a prepared script. Create stories, make up five or ten different explanations for something that you did, believing each one as you tell it. You might at first think that this is lying, but soon you will discover that sticking to the same story because it is the "true" story is not only lying, but deadening.

People have senses to see, hear, and feel what is around them, not to make sense of things. Stories preempt the senses by defining what people see, hear, and feel. Stories are representations, not the things they represent. Language can be a blessing or a curse, depending on whether it is believed or enjoyed. Tell stories for fun, not for justification.

Cake Six

When you give up your career, you will discover what your career is. When you give up who you perceive yourself to be, you will discover who you are. When you give up the tiny piece of turf you have been fighting for for so long, Earth and the universe will become you, they always were. Now your real career is that of a philosopher. A philosopher doesn't do much but think. Thinking and doing don't go together well. A philosopher is to be taken care of, and to have so little responsibility that thought comes first. You are a philosopher, just not a very good or honest one. A philosopher who denies being one will not be true to his or her profession. Time will be wasted, and thought will be used for anything but philosophy. When you quit your career, and then all careers, you will discover that you are a philosopher. You will have the intelligence of a philosopher, as you constantly give up all you know for what you can learn, and then give that up too.

You don't have to give up things—just anything you perceive you have some special relationship to. By special relationship, I mean that you own it, like it, love it, see it, smell it, or know it. All of these are dependent on perception, at least, initially. Thus, the special perception must be released. Give up labels. Quit knowing, understanding, and even being. These, I think, are often easy to quit, because so much quitting has taken place to get to this deep and wide level of quitting that quitting is no longer suspect as a path to freedom, self-discovery, and light at this level.

You have to give up love to love, and being loved to be loved. You have to quit to see. Only the blind can see, because only the blind can value sight. It is the way you hold onto something that determines your relationship to it. Anything that you are holding onto you will soon confuse with who you are. Stripping that thing of all value, as it becomes you, and *seems* to become more valuable. Remember, in a game, what isn't is more important than what is. So what you already possess, including yourself, is less important than all that isn't. Demeaning, isn't it? Your current philosophy, or lack of one, has led you to where you are, but it can't take you much farther. That is, in fact, its purpose—to not take you much farther, to slow you down and tether you at every point, to blind you while leaving you with sight. Explore yourself as a philosopher. Once you have quit those other careers, you will discover the process of letting go of thought so fundamental to being a philosopher.

The roots of philosophy are in questioning everything, and discovering anything that you are currently not questioning, then questioning that too. To be a philosopher is to give up knowing where you stand for uncertainty, and then giving up uncertainty too. Anything you are holding is released, allowing you to see it. You are nearsighted, too much so for any glasses to correct your condition. Being nearsighted is having anything that is closer to you look bigger than that which is farther away. Your whole method of perception comes into question, since it is so egotistical. Perspective must be questioned; because location determines size for you, it makes you very big and everything else very small. No wonder you think you are so important, or unimportant; it is the same thing. Both require you to think of yourself, and perceive other things, from the perspective that you call yourself, misleading at worst, crazy at best.

Question what matters to you, when you get the courage, because questioning what doesn't matter to you is a waste of time and energy. The first step in quitting what matters to you is to discover what matters to you. You have to give up anything that matters to you, and then give up having nothing matter to you by having something matter to you. This process takes you full circle, and the faster you can do it the more apt you are to reach escape velocity, to get out of the loop and *wave* goodbye to all that you have held to and perceived yourself to be. Light is a wave, and, as you recognize yourself as a wave, you will discover that your surroundings are constantly new, and that it is you who reveals their newness. It is you who is born each moment. You didn't come into this world with anything, and you won't leave it with anything, so why hold so tightly to things in between? There is an honesty in the beginning and in the end that is often lost so thoroughly in the middle that life is not worth living. Quitting returns you to both end and beginning at the same time. It demolishes all that is made up in between.

When you are returned to both the end and beginning at the same time, what is revealed are two more illusions, the beginning and the end—which you get to give up. People hold to death when there is no such thing. Two things are for certain, death and taxes. You don't have to pay taxes if you don't earn anything, and you don't have to die if you are not holding to anything. Light never ends, and you don't either. Quit death before it is too late. Philosophers never die. Is Socrates dead? Is Plato dead? It all depends on what you mean by dead. Is Christ dead? It is you who determines what lives and dies. If you think of Christ, Christ is alive in that moment of thought. And if you hold to your perception of Christ, Christ dies again. Once more crucified by you. The same is true for everyone and everything you perceive. If you see something once, it lives for you. If you perceive it twice, you live for it, it dies, and you die with it.

It is your perceptions that you have to quit. It is the repetition that you call life. Any perception is fresh and new until it is repeated. As a philosopher, when you question you invite yourself to let go, you open up and discover that you are not who you thought you were, neither are you your thoughts.

You are a *thinking* being; a philosopher, not a consumer. Your role is to think, and anything that gets in the way of your thinking is to be questioned and discarded, quit. Nothing can get in the way of your thought unless you hold to it. It is not matter; it is mattering that you must let go of. Anything that matters to you rules you. If you can give up the mattering; then you don't have to give up that which matters. Mattering is a static state of mind, a dam, blocking the flow that is you. Giving up matter takes time and energy, while giving up mattering gives time and energy.

To enjoy this breath fully, you must forfeit the next one. If you focus on the next one, you will surely suffocate while missing the pleasure of this one. As a philosopher, you must quit. You must let go of anything that you hold to. Life becomes a release as you reveal that which is around you rather than sticking to it. You become lighter as you perceive, rather than holding to, your perception.

You have confused perception with control, and control with perception. What you see is what you see, it is not what you *think* you see. What you think is just what you think, a tiny subset of what you can think. The bigger this subset becomes, the bigger you become, and perception is used as a tool of expansion. What you know always gets in the way of what you don't. Do you want what you are holding in your hand or what is behind door number one? Remember, a bird in the hand is worth two in the bush. Or is it?

Hold on to what you know, because it is the most scarce, rare commodity in the universe. Let go of what you know and you will discover yourself as a philosopher.

Cake Seven

There is so much to quit. But there is also all the time in the world to quit. What's your hurry? Give up time, space will go with it. Anything that is dependent on something else isn't much use. There is no space without time, thus both must be illusion. Relax, there is nothing to do, and all the time in the world to do it. Quit time. Let go of the past and the future. Nothing is immortal; you can't lose it and it can't lose you. Attempts to the contrary are futile and have you convinced that you are wasting time. Wasting what there isn't, isn't very wasteful.

Evolution is a euphemism for time. It is the threat of science. Quit consciousness laughing at evolution. Morality is the threat of the ages. There are so many threats around. Threats are warnings about possible futures. Threats lead to fear. What might happen? What could happen? When you quit time, there will be no future to worry about, and no past to fall back on. Free fall is the only way to be free. Soon you will discover that you are not falling at all. Falling on Earth happens at thirty-two feet per second squared, not nearly the speed of light no matter how long you fall. Light is too light to fall. It can be bent a bit and remain light, but it will not tolerate any slowing down. What if you didn't tolerate any slowing down? What if you wouldn't put up with having any thought more than once?

When you begin moving at the speed of light, you will realize there is nowhere to go. It will dawn on you that life is not hard, that there is nothing hard about light. Your role as light is to reveal and then reveal again. You don't get to stay in any one place for any time at all; you dissipate and spend no time everywhere. Now, that is good fun. You can play all the time, if you quit. If you then quit playing, you will discover new layers of play. Once you start quitting, without replacing what you have quit, you will shed your skin. You will be unprotected and won't need protection. You will be bigger than you thought possible and won't need to know where you stand, because knowing where you stand presupposes that there are places you don't stand. Light can go anywhere, and anywhere is only revealed as somewhere when life has been and gone. Light has to strike an object and then leave that object for you to even see. If light is absorbed, it disappears. Light comes and goes. You just want to come without going. You want to hold on, and when you do so everything disappears. You become absorbed in that which you perceive.

The lack of satisfaction you call life that always follows this process is unnecessary and unnatural. Playing is coming and quitting is going. Both are necessary; and the closer together you can get the two, the more life you will have. When they occur at the same time, you finally will be fast enough to see reality. You will be free. You will have given up your last stumbling block—fear. Fear, again, presupposes that you are less than you are, that you could lose something.

The universe does not have a lost and found, but it does have a lot of collectors. It has hoards of hoarders. To hamster something, you have to consider that there is too little to go around. There is too much to go around, that is the problem. There is so much to go around that you will always have an abundance of everything. You call this abundance shortage, but what's in a name? You quit naming a while ago, didn't you?

The universe is discontinuous; everything is lost, and then everything is found. This lost and found happens everywhere all the time. Quitting brings you closer to simulating this natural rhythm. Quitting is the most honest thing you can do. It ends illusion and returns you to where you always were, but with the perception of yourself as the universe. You have never lost, but you perceive that you lose. You have never found, but you perceive that you have found. Your perceptions will mislead you, but less so if they are not repeated. Quit repetition, and you will discover yourself as creative beyond your wildest dreams. You live and die in each moment, unless you attempt to carry something from moment to moment. If you do that, then you enter a world of make-believe in which you are an actor, a character playing a role, being directed by everything outside yourself, and not being paid at all.

Cut

Take two. There you are standing over a coffin that contains, a) your father, b) your pet dog Sparky, c) an image of who you used to be, d) a crusty piece of cheese resting on a check made out to you, the dollar amount unreadable without your glasses. What you do next is not in the script. You lean back, inhaling and stretching as many muscles as you can without forcing any of them.

Cut

Take three. There you are standing on the end of a long diving board. You are poised for a jump, uncharacteristically cognizant of the board under your feet. You never know how much you are holding until the opportunity to release is presented. You begin to lean forward, but catch yourself, just in time, just in space, just in the games of the human race. You look away from the diving board and back over your shoulder. You wonder if what you will do in the future will really prove out all the things you have done in the past. If you had to sum up that past in just one word, that word would have to be…

Cut

Take four. The camera pans in on you in bed. Not an unflattering angle, but not an angel either. What a difference order makes. There you are lying without covers; you wouldn't need covers if you weren't lying. You see yourself as you are, afraid that you are, but right next to that is another picture of you as you really are. It is difficult to hold both of these. One looms so large, not the right one. The other, who you really are, seems too tiny to attend to. You try to jump into one of the two pictures; which one?

Cut

Take five. It is expensive, but we will keep shooting until we can get something that makes sense here, and just might convince others to come to the theater. How easy can life get? Another test: a) So easy that you wouldn't even have to believe it. b) As easy as it is now. c) As easy as you want it to be. d) No easier than the most difficult math problem you have ever had to attempt to solve.

Cut

Take six. Will the tests never end? You are invited to a grand party. Everyone will be there except maybe you, depending on your answer to the following riddle. Hey diddle diddle, the cat and the fiddle, the cow jumped over the moon. The little dog laughed to see such sport, and the dish ran away with the _____. If you fill in the blank correctly, you can come to the party as long as you, a) have something nice to wear, b) can find an escort who is a lot like you, c) can afford it, d) don't talk about the past while you are at the party. If you filled in the blank with something funny (that at least made you laugh), you can come to the party and entertain. If you couldn't figure out what went in the blank at all, you can come and work at the party, serving drinks perhaps or cleaning up the kitchen.

Cut

Scene seven. At the party. You walk in, dressed to the nines. What will you do next?

"*Introduction to Spiritual Harmony* is witty, wise, humorous, and sometimes exasperatingly truthful—not unlike the Deity Herself. The author's dialogues with God sparkle with intelligence and humor.

We feel encouraged to carry on our own."

Matthew Fox

Matthew Fox is an internationally known lecturer and author. His latest book is *The Reinvention of Work: A New Vision of Livelihood for Our Time* (HarperSanFrancisco).

"You don't have to agree with Stocking's God to be challenged and enlightened. Learn who you really are and about the true meaning of God and the place God takes in our lives.

A very interesting book."

Bernie S. Siegel, M.D.

Bernie Siegel is the author of *Love, Medicine & Miracles, Peace, Love and Healing* and *How To Live Between Office Visits*.

Introduction to Spiritual Harmony

Imagine that you are sitting across from God. What are your five questions for God? The answers to your questions may be waiting for you in **Introduction to Spiritual Harmony**. What would life be like if you could celebrate and delight in waking, breathing, moving, and thinking?

How would life be if you could celebrate everything?

Books by Jerry Stocking

Cognitive Harmony, An Adventure in Mental Fitness
There are No Accidents, A Magical Love Story
Introduction to Spiritual Harmony
Enlightenment is Losing Your Mind

Contact Moose Ear Press, or A Choice Experience, Inc. to find out about quantity discounts or information on other books, seminars, or tapes by Jerry Stocking.

Moose Ear Press
A Choice Experience, Inc.

PO Box 335
Chetek, WI 54728

715-924-4906
FAX 715-924-4738

To receive the Epilogue to *How to Win By Quitting* please send $1.00 to:

How to Win By Quitting Epilogue
Moose Ear Press
PO Box 335
Chetek, WI 54728

or Call: 715-924-4906